How to
Manage your own block of flats
Second Edition

A flat-owner's guide to taking and maintaining control

John Cumming
Richard Hickie

No responsibility for loss occasioned to any person acting or refraining from action as a result of the material in this publication can be accepted.

Second edition October 2004
First published November 1993

© The College of Estate Management 2004

ISBN 1 904388 31 0

Published by
The College of Estate Management
Whiteknights, Reading RG6 6AW

CONTENTS

Chapter   *Page*

Introduction   1

PART 1

1. **Getting organised**   7
2. **Right to Manage companies**   15
3. **The company, its directors and their duties**   30
4. **The responsibilities of management and running meetings**   51
5. **Managerial and professional advice and advisers**   63
6. **The lease and service charges**   77
7. **Problems associated with buildings**   91

PART 2

8. **Assessing resources and setting objectives**   105
9. **Planning strategy**   124
10. **Lessees, subtenants and other residents: problems and solutions**   138
11. **Building contracts and specifications**   162
12. **Managing the future**   172

    Appendix 1:   The Annual General Meeting   188
    Appendix 2A: Building works and the refurbishment of flats   190
    Appendix 2B: Standard Conditions for Contractors   195
    Appendix 3:   Welcome Pack and House Rules   198
    Appendix 4:   Formal notice requiring access   201

DETAILED CONTENTS

Chapter		Page
	Introduction	1
	Four block personalities	2
	The advantages and disadvantages of 'experience'	3
	Some basic assumptions	4
	About this book	5
1	**Getting organised**	7
	Reviewing what you manage	7
	Why have you decided to buy/manage it?	8
	The scope of the task	9
	Action	14
	Reference	14
2	**Right to Manage companies**	15
	The new relationship between the RTM and landlord	15
	A checklist prior to 'acquisition'	17
	Check the information you need to help you manage	17
	Service charges held by the landlord	18
	Deciding what to do about the landlord's existing contracts	19
	The legal position	19
	Transfer of staff	20
	Understanding the scope of your new powers	20
	The Lease	
	The Memorandum and Articles of Association	
	Memorandum of Association of an RTM company	
	Articles of Association of an RTM company	
	Managing the property	22
	Responsibilities not transferred to the RTM company	23
	Forfeiture and repossession	24
	Approvals	28
	Action	29
	Prior to the acquisition date	
	References	29
3	**The company, its directors and their duties**	30
	Alternative structures of accountability	30
	Information from Companies House for smaller companies	31
	The company	32
	Legal documents	
	The Certificate of Incorporation	
	The Memorandum of Association	

The Articles of Association	
Amendments to the Memorandum and Articles of Association	33
Company rules and non-members	34
Limited liability	34
Company assets	35
Corporate structure and accountability	36
The theory	
The reality	
The first company meeting as landlord	38
Deciding on management structure	
Appointing the full board of directors	
The appointment of directors	
The appointment of a chairman	
The appointment of the company secretary	
Other directors	
Directors' duties	44
House code of conduct for directors	46
Company stationery	47
Registered office	47
Statutory obligations of Industrial and Provident Societies	48
Action	49
As a company director or shareholder	
As a member of an Industrial and Provident Society	
Reading	50

4 **The responsibilities of management and running meetings** 51

Meetings	52
Advantages and disadvantages of meetings	
The importance of good chairmanship	52
Committee procedure	53
Types of meeting	54
Shareholders' meetings (Annual General Meetings)	
Directors' meetings	
Defining the authority and activities of committees	58
The management committee	
Management committee membership	
Running management committee meetings	
The absolute importance of courteous behaviour at meetings	62
Action	62

5 **Managerial and professional advice and advisers** 63
    The managing agent 64

      Choosing a managing agent
      Managing a managing agent
      Delegating responsibility to the managing agent
      Assessing the work of the managing agent
  Deciding whether you need professional advice   70
  Different types of professional adviser   71
      The accountant
      The solicitor
      The surveyor
      The insurance broker
  Choosing a professional – the benefits   74
  Professional fees   75
  Action   75
  Reading   76

6   The lease and service charges   77
  The start of a lease   77
  Problems with leases   78
  Making variations to the lease   78
  Understanding the lease   79
      'Traditional' and 'modern' leases
      Understanding the contents of a modern lease
      The older lease format
  Service charges   83
      What can be charged for
      Calculating the charge
      Allocating the charge
      Further legal requirements
      Service charge disputes and Leasehold Valuation Tribunals
      Consulting the leaseholders
      Trust status of service charges
      Service charge policy – managerial implications
  Action   90
  Reading   90

7   Problems associated with buildings   91
  Water damage by flooding from an adjacent flat   92
  Dampness   92
      Causes of dampness
  Types of dampness   93
      Creeping dampness
      Burst pipes
      Storms and damage by the elements
      Brickwork-related problems

      Rising damp
      Condensation
   Immediate action against dampness 98
   Consequences of dampness 99
      Dry rot
      Preventing dry rot
   Structural problems 101
   Timber 102
   Action 103
   Reading 104

8 Assessing resources and setting objectives 105
   Resources 105
      Service charges
      The reserve fund
      Rents
      Expertise
      Existing staff
      Reliable contractors and tradesmen
      Professionals
   Additional important information 110
      From the former managing agent
      From the local authority
   Aims and objectives 112
      Development of the property
      Managerial performance (managing agent)
      Income and expenditure
      Planned maintenance
      Staff
      Amenities and services
   Setting objectives 116
   Getting consent for objectives 118
      Transferable vote
      The LIP model
   Constraints on objectives 122
   Action 123

9 Planning strategy 124
   Why devise a plan? 124
   Planning 125
   Creating the rolling plan 126
      Development of the property
         Refurbishments
         Major Projects
      Maintenance

        Planned Maintenance
        Maintenance Contracts
     Property Repairs
     Staff
     Amenities
     Other Costs

Costs	132
The role of planning in a lessee-owned company	133
The reserve fund (or sinking fund)	134
The project based approach	136
Comparing the three approaches to planning	137
Action	137

10 Lessees, subtenants and other residents: problems and solutions — 138

Directors' duty of care – confused with 'caring'	139
The value of the 'tenant's pack'	139
Abuse of leases by leaseholders	141
The unintentional offender	
More difficult leaseholders	
Abuse of lease by subtenants	144
Buy to let – rent for profit	145
New residents	147
Concerning alterations to flats	147
Drainage	
Communality vs privacy	149
Responding to disputes between leaseholders	150
Security of cost	150
Serious problems and difficult cases	151
Bad payers and non-payers	151
The sequence of formal letters	152
Forfeiture	155
Financial leverage against bad payers	156
Hardship cases	157
Conflict	158
Should the company get involved?	
Constructive conflict	160
Compromise vs collaboration	160
Action	161
Reading	161

11 Building contracts and specifications — 162

Before the contract	162
Choosing a surveyor	
Scaffolding contracts	

The first contract	164
Forms of contract	
Stages in preparing and carrying out a contract	166
The specification	
Preliminaries and contract particulars	
Preambles or materials and workmanship	
The works	
Setting up and running the contract	167
How the works are supervised	169
Payment	169
Action	171
Reading	171

12 Managing the future   172

Implementing decisions	173
Managing the service charge and accounts	174
Managing staff	175
Pay	
Performance	
Contracts of employment	
Duties	
Materials and equipment	
Communications with staff	
Managing Health and Safety	178
Information on Health and Safety	
Fire hazards and precautions	180
Notifying residents	
Managing maintenance and service contracts	182
Pest control	
Insurance	
Boiler (central heating and hot water)	
Lift	
Planned maintenance	
Managing residents' matters and amenities	184
Irregularities of occupancy	
Security	
Amenities	
Conclusion	187
Reading	187
Appendix 1: **The Annual General Meeting**	188
Appendix 2A: **Building works and the refurbishment of flats**	190
Appendix 2B: **Standard Conditions for Contractors**	195
Appendix 3: **Welcome Pack and House Rules**	198
Appendix 4: **Formal notice requiring access**	201

ACKNOWLEDGEMENTS

In writing this book we have drawn substantially on the considerable experience we have gained from working in harness with many resident-owned and managed blocks of flats in South West London. To these we acknowledge our debt in passing on to others the benefits of that experience.

We wish to thank Miriam Lambert of the National Housing Federation for providing us with valuable assistance concerning the rules of Industrial and Provident Societies. Robert Levene of the Federation of Private Residents' Associations plied us liberally with useful information. Jane Barry read and made useful suggestions on the new chapter on Right to Manage companies. We remember with affection the late Geoff Day whose insights and experience helped shape the Introduction. We are grateful again to Valerie Cumming for applying her proof-reading skills to the second edition.

Peter Blake and Anita Akin of the College of Estate Management were patient and understanding during our attempts to unearth the most recent government information. Our thanks are also due to our editor Martine Peacock and Jeanne Bradbury who has provided a comprehensive and much improved index.

Finally, we acknowledge and thank Mira Bar Hillel who prompted the initial idea for this book and Peter Haler of LEASE who urged the second edition.

JLC
RAH

FOR

VC

and

AH

FOREWORD

At the Leasehold Advisory Service we provide a great amount of advice to flat-owners on how to take control of their buildings and constantly refer clients to the first edition of *How to Manage Your Own Block of Flats*. We are delighted to welcome this revised edition which we consider essential reading for any flat-owner.

Various Governments have provided the means for groups of flat-owners to buy the freeholds of their buildings and, more recently, simply to take over the management from the landlord. However, after completion of the purchase or the assumption of the management rights, the legislation provides little further guidance and the successful flat-owners are left wondering, 'What now?' Running even a small block of flats is no easy matter; a major block represents a sizeable business and is not something to be taken on lightly. Just because one is a flat-owner does not necessarily imply one has a natural gift toward the complexities of financial, structural and legal issues facing the manager. The legislation that provides rights and protections for leasehold flat-owners also imposes strict and time-consuming responsibilities and liabilities upon the manager, with significant implications to cash flows. The essential task of the leaseholder-manager must be in maintaining the financial health of the block, balancing the books, and this will be dependent on the ability to ensure the proper levying and collection of service charges, without falling foul of the maze of regulations and statutory requirements.

This book provides a sensible and friendly approach to all the aspects of management – legal, technical and financial – including the absolute necessity of dealing with each other. It is not a technical manual for 'management anoraks'; it sets out what a prospective or existing leaseholder-manager needs to know, the choices to be made and checklists for action. It will be equally relevant to those taking on the responsibility of management and those who choose to employ a professional manager, in setting out the basic machinery of company operation and decision-making and the issues to be faced in maintaining the structure in which they live.

Peter Haler
Chief Executive
Leasehold Advisory Service (LEASE)

PREFACE TO THE SECOND EDITION

In the decade or so before we wrote the first edition of *How to Manage Your Own Block of Flats*, groups of leaseholders organised themselves to take control of their own blocks of flats largely on an ad hoc basis. Chinfort Ltd (Resident Association Management), which we set up in the late 1970s, assisted many such groups to form companies in order to buy out their freeholds. Freehold purchases by groups of flat-owners were almost always the result of dissatisfaction and disagreements with the existing landlord. This intensely hands-on experience, the setting up of individual leaseholder companies and the managing of the properties, often from a condition of visible dilapidation to a good state of repair and appearance, became the subject matter of our first edition.

It was the Leasehold Reform, Housing and Urban Development Act 1993 which prompted that first edition and while the then limited market became flooded with advice on how to buy your block of flats, this was the only title which started where they left off and looked at the wider and continuing problems of staffing, building maintenance, refurbishment contracts, formal meetings, dealing with difficult residents, management resources and planning, in other words, the management of the company and its property.

As a result of the Commonhold and Leasehold Reform Act 2002 (CLRA) many more groups of residents have become eligible to take control of the management of their own buildings without first having to go to the expense of purchasing the freehold. The new Chapter 2 in this edition is specifically written as an introduction for Right to Manage companies.

In the intervening ten years, since the first edition was published, much has changed within this field. The central body for advice and information is the Leasehold Advisory Service (LEASE), the grant-aided independent agency set up by the government. The Association of Residential Managing Agents (ARMA) and the Federation of Private Residents' Associations (FPRA) have both developed as authoritative bodies serving the movement towards better resident-managed blocks. But the greatest change is the impact of the new legislation, CLRA, and the additional detailed administrative systems that it requires of lessee-owned companies. This necessarily refocuses the book and while we hope to retain a hands-on, in-house, businesslike approach, in this new edition we have included more managerial considerations, emphasising the importance of professional advice and advisers.

This is a starter book for what we believe is a developing modern movement among flat-owners. It is for all who intend to do what many others have already done, namely, manage their own block of flats and involve themselves, in the words of the subtitle of this book, in 'taking and maintaining control'.

JLC
RAH
Battersea
June 2004

INTRODUCTION

This book provides a basic introduction for flat-owners who are involved, or becoming involved, in managing their own blocks of flats. It takes as its starting point the position of a leaseholder or group of leaseholders who have already set up a company and obtained the ownership or through the terms of their lease, the management of the building – or in the case of a Right to Manage company, have taken over the administration of their block. From this point on the book concerns the business of managing a resident-run building.

Flats are usually managed through companies run by flat-owners in one of five ways:

- Right to Enfranchise (RTE) company
- Commonhold company
- Freehold buyout – resident management company
- A management company set up under the terms of the lease
- Right to Manage (RTM) company.

The main difference between these companies, as far as this book is concerned, is that the first three own the freehold of the property they manage, and are therefore the landlord in every respect, the fourth one manages but might also own, whereas the last one is a management company only and while it will exercise most of the landlord's rights and duties in law, the landlord remains the freeholder.

Although the Commonhold and Leasehold Reform Act 2002 introduces commonhold as a new form of land tenure in England and Wales, most experts believe that it will be a very long time before it has a substantial impact on the nature of residential property ownership. Most professionals in the field will be happier with existing legislation and management methods which have already been tried and tested. Residents who choose to go down the commonhold route will find the authoritative publications of the Leasehold Advisory Service (LEASE) valuable sources of information as the implementation of legislation develops in this field. However, this book is relevant to those who choose or buy in to commonhold ownership, with the exception of particular differences, for example those relating to the administration of service charges.

So, whether you run a large block and intend to appoint a managing agent and other professionals to do the job for you, or have taken on the

Introduction

management of a smaller block or house conversion and intend to adopt the 'hands-on' approach, this book is for you.

Managing your own block of flats is much the same as managing anything else. The same principles apply. It is different from running a house only in so far as it is a bigger job. The building itself is bigger; there are more people to communicate with; and it involves handling larger amounts of money. But there is now a body of knowledge, derived specifically from this practice, which provides the subject matter for much of this book.

The book also attempts to respond to the need to demystify and state clearly and simply matters which are often thought to be the sole domain of the professional. An understanding of buildings, of the professionals who serve them, and of appropriate management methods, enables most people who are used to taking responsibility in other fields of work, to manage their own block of flats.

Throughout the text, and for the sake of simplicity, the masculine pronoun has been used. The active and successful involvement of women as directors in lessee-owned companies does not need this book as an advocate. It is unusual to find an all-male board. The use of 'he' throughout simply recognises a somewhat inadequate convention.

Four block personalities

There are almost as many types of resident-managed company as there are buildings that are managed by their residents. The examples below are not to be thought of as necessarily good models, nor do they constitute anything like an exhaustive list. They are convenient examples which serve to show why different blocks are run in different ways.

> *Type A*
> The large block which sees itself as a 'prestige' building and likes to think that service charges, though substantial, are not generally a burden or an issue. It is looked after by a managing agent who reports periodically to the board or a management committee, largely made up of people who are often decision-makers in their own chosen careers.
>
> *Type B*
> The purpose-built block in a less prestigious location with a self-image similar to Type A but because of historical problems, prefers to instruct a managing agent, meets regularly, and likes to feel it has a 'hands-on' approach through its frequent meetings with the agent.

> *Type C*
> The substantial building with no managing agent whose board of directors prefers to allocate responsibilities and functions through a management committee. It is cost conscious, meets regularly, and appoints professionals when required.
>
> *Type D*
> The smaller property, ten flats or fewer, with no managing agent, run on a less formal basis with a minimum of shared services. It prefers ad hoc meetings and is often centred on one or two lessees who are interested in the task of running the company.

The advantages and disadvantages of 'experience'

Some management committees in resident-managed blocks (but certainly not all) have a wide range of expertise at their disposal with sound managerial experience. This can be both a benefit and a liability. The benefits generally arise from experienced managers not being at all daunted by the size of the job; they organise or run a block of flats with a budget often smaller than that for which they are responsible in their normal working life. The disadvantage, however, derives from a general belief among many successful managers that if a thing works well in their experience elsewhere, then it is perfectly adequate when managing a block of flats.

Another false assumption is the one that goes: 'If I have lived in this property for some length of time, then I am an expert in the matter of what is best for it.' While the knowledge of the experienced manager can be of value in the resident management company, that of the aspiring amateur surveyor is much less so and ill-informed decisions can be very expensive.

However, an experienced manager on a lessee management committee may also become impatient when he feels that his freely given advice is not accepted unquestioningly. Surprisingly, and innocently, he is often the one that forgets to remember which committee he is sitting on, and that he is not among colleagues of the same calibre, paid by the same company, in similar career structures, who know how to use meetings to advance the interests of their own departments. Instead he is helping to run a block of flats in the overall interest of the lessee/shareholders and may frequently be disarmed by the frankness and honesty of people who believe that he can be wrong.

Introduction

Management literature is full of knowing and opinionated gurus telling you 'How I created Success out of a Failure', implying that if you take their advice you can do the same. But you are not running a car hire firm or a sportswear factory. Your method of wealth generation will be different, your shareholders have different expectations and needs, and you are in very different markets (labour, financial, supplier, contractor, professional). You are also, as a company, very much smaller. It is clear that you do not have to be an expert in Chaos Theory to understand that one of the first principles you must apply is: 'Assess the business on its own merits'.

It is worth remembering at the outset that everybody is equally new to one another as well as to the business of running a lessee-owned company. Going through the prescribed legal steps of setting up a management company is a very different process from the human business of managing it. The first has been done successfully, the second you are about to embark upon. In a fairly short time, once the objectives and plan have been agreed, the new management team can be working effectively. Individuals frequently become quite expert in their chosen specialisms, begin to ask the right searching questions and understand the often quite detailed answers.

Some basic assumptions

Managing a residential property is a business. It may be non-profit-making, but it must not make a loss. You will be using the same tools as most businesses, but to a different end.

Three main assumptions are basic to the understanding of the uniqueness of this kind of enterprise. Even though its decisions and actions are as strictly bound by the constraints of law and lease, these assumptions make the activities of a lessee-owned company significantly different from the activities of a conventional landlord. They may be presented as follows.

> 1 The business objectives and plan for implementing them will be generated and controlled from inside the building by the lessee-owned company, which alone will be responsible for policy.
>
> 2 All the important decisions about the property will in future be made mainly in the interests of flat-owners and to the benefit of those in residence.

> 3   It is not company policy that the property will be developed to be sold for profit in the future. (While this may seem obvious, the advice professional advisers give will need to recognise this fact.)

It is not the intention here to provide the perfect model for running your own company. You will have the last word on that. The purpose of this book is to help you recognise and evaluate your own resources, set appropriate objectives, plan and put the plan into action and get on with the running of your own block. There are no quick fixes if you are doing the management yourself, but there are better and worse ways of doing it. And when you have done it, there is a considerable sense of personal satisfaction and shared achievement.

About this book

The book is in two parts.

Part One reviews the background against which you will be managing your property.

Chapter 1, *'Getting organised'*, contains a general review of what you have taken on and allows you to stand back, review and assess the reasons why you want to manage the property.

Chapter 2, *'Right to Manage companies'*, is for management companies who do not buy their freehold and which are set up under the Commonhold and Leasehold Reform Act 2002 in order to take over the management of their property. To avoid duplication, other chapters are referred to where matters common to all resident management companies are dealt with.

Chapter 3 is an introduction to *'The company, its directors and their duties'* and looks at the nature and functions of a company and the duties of directors. It also provides an outline description of an Industrial and Provident Society.

Chapter 4, *'The responsibilities of management and running meetings'*, discusses forms of management structure found in resident-run blocks, how they tie in to the decision-making and reporting relationships, and why particular models are appropriate in some circumstances while inappropriate in others.

Chapter 5, *'Managerial and professional advice and advisers'*, covers the appointment and management of a managing agent and looks at the nature of professional advice, how to use it, and the range of professional bodies and advice available.

Introduction

Chapter 6, *'The lease and service charges'*, takes the reader through an outline of the lease and, as far as possible, attempts to decipher and discover the meanings of its various parts.

Chapter 7, *'Problems associated with buildings'*, introduces the building itself and especially the most common causes of damage and deterioration to fabric found in large residential buildings.

Part Two addresses the business of management.

Chapter 8, *'Assessing resources and setting objectives'*, and Chapter 9, *'Planning strategy'*, apply practical management methods to the management of residential lessee-owned companies. They cover identifying and evaluating resources, deciding upon and setting objectives, planning and putting the plan into action.

Chapter 10 is a special chapter on *'Lessees, subtenants and other residents: problems and solutions'*, and provides an overview of, and suggests possible remedies for, some familiar people problems.

Chapter 11, *'Building contracts and specifications'*, looks at standard approaches to getting building work done and discusses forms of contract, specifications, redecoration contracts and working with surveyors on the block itself.

Finally, Chapter 12, *'Managing the future'*, attempts to coordinate the substance of the whole book in order to provide a simple programme of meetings and reporting systems so that things may get done with least fuss on a continuing basis.

The *Appendices* are there in the main to help you to order your thoughts at certain points in the text. Some of them are model letters, others are checklists. Their significance is explained in the text.

PART ONE

CHAPTER 1

Getting organised

This chapter provides a simple framework against which you can appraise your present position. The company has been set up. Some irksome matters may still be outstanding, but you have arrived at a position where you share responsibility for a residential complex of large, medium or small proportions which requires managing. The responsible body, the company, has been legally constituted and the first major objective you set yourselves, has been achieved. Now the matter of managing the property must be addressed.

The same basic managerial principles apply to running a block of flats as to anything else. The difference is that you are applying them to an unfamiliar set of circumstances for which you may need to develop contacts with a range of professional advisers. However, it is useful to be clear about what advice you need and why you need it. The first activity, therefore, is to identify and describe the task in hand. This chapter aims to help you stand back and assess your particular circumstances and think into the role of block management.

Reviewing what you manage

Having spent all your time focusing your attention on setting up the company, seeking information and, at times, settling differences with the 'other side', you now have to make an important adjustment. Insofar as you now control the property, the 'other side' no longer exists (excepting RTM companies, see Chapter 2). Within the bounds of lawfulness, available finances and neighbourly consent, you can enjoy the brief relaxation of a honeymoon period reviewing the situation and planning for the future. This frequently reported phenomenon is associated with the 'Independence Day Effect', a euphoric condition experienced by those who mistakenly believe that they are now free to do what they like with their building. What you *can* do is prescribed in your Lease and Memorandum and Articles of Association (see Chapter 3).

Getting organised

A block of flats run by its residents can be described in terms of its *attributes*. For example:

- A sizeable property
- A multiple residence
- A financial asset
- A legal entity
- A home
- A source of income
- An employer
- A provider of services and amenities
- A user of public services and amenities
- ... And other features peculiar to your property.

The property can also be described in terms of *what you want it to be*. The most useful questions that can be asked here concern why you are involved in the management of a substantial property.

Why have you decided to buy/manage it?

The reasons most frequently given by resident companies for having collectively decided to manage their own residential blocks through a jointly owned management company are:

- To obtain security of tenure
- To control leasehold/freehold problems
- To get rid of a bad landlord
- To control erratic maintenance expenditure
- To control contracts
- To restore order where leases are being abused
- To improve the value of the property
- To economise
- To go upmarket
- To be able to stay where they are
- To control the destiny of the block.

Review your reasons for setting up the management company together as a group of company members. Set these down in an agreed order so the reasons why the management company was set up are clear and agreed by all, especially the order in which you want to do things. Otherwise, at some point in the future, when a rather large sum of money is being allocated for roof repairs or a full boiler service, you will hear a member of the managing committee say, 'I thought when we took on the management of this block we decided to do things in a different order.' A number of people present will not recall that particular version but will begin to disagree among themselves as to what actually was agreed. The result can be confusion and delay and the first big disagreement. This is a very familiar and frequent occurrence. The roof will have to wait until everybody agrees a new set of priorities, and the new reasons given for them will be quite different from those you yourself recollect as the original reasons.

It is better, at this stage, to know you can rely on the certainty of an agreed and written set of criteria when important decisions have to be made and priorities need to be asserted. So this should be an early objective of the management committee.

A clear set of priorities should also help to identify any skills you may need to call upon when you come to look later at the make-up of the management team. The management team is the group that will be making the decisions on a regular basis, be it the board of directors alone, a management committee, or something that develops quite naturally within a reporting system between it and the main body of lessee/shareholders.

The scope of the task

You must try to create an effective management team (see Chapter 4) that reflects the size and type of residential complex. It will bear the legal and managerial responsibilities for:

- Carrying out company business
- Collecting service charges
- Collecting ground rent
- Employing contractors
- Insuring the property
- Employing the staff (caretakers and cleaners)
- Communicating with lessee/shareholders

- Instructing the managing agents where appointed
- Carrying out the landlord's covenants under the lease
- Ensuring lessees abide by their covenants under the lease
- Managing services and amenities – car parks, lifts, TV aerials, gardens, etc.

The management body should be able to cope with formal and informal problems of consent and compliance. You will want to be able to bring people together in the sense that one is approaching a joint venture. It requires an ability to communicate with all the residents in the building. But you may also have to flex the managerial muscles when you have to tackle a disruptive resident and it is at times like these that a sense of community is a support to the board. How this develops will depend to a large extent on what sort of block you have and such considerations as:

- **The history of the block.** Has it been well managed in the past? Has it undergone any particular alterations? Does it have any long-standing problems or particular needs?

- **The size of the block.** Larger blocks will frequently be more impersonal and will require a greater emphasis on written communication or notice boards. Blocks of different sizes will pose different maintenance and service related problems.

- **Available expertise among lessee/shareholders.** Do you have any resident solicitors, surveyors, accountants, trained PR or marketing professionals who might be willing to contribute professional expertise and experience?

- **Location of the building.** Could you share facilities with neighbouring buildings? Does the location of the block imply special management needs (for example, is it in a conservation area)? Will residents be 'image conscious'?

- **Age mix of tenants.** Old and young have less money than middle-class, middle-aged professionals. Those who have bought recently (of whatever age) have higher mortgages and will not want high service charges at the outset.

- **How many flats are leased back to the previous landlord, and how many flats are let by lessees to subtenants?** This will affect the number of residents who actually have a say in the running of the company: their attitude to management and expenditure will be different from those who do not.

- **The recent history of difficult tenancies.** There might be urgent people problems that must be quickly cleared up – they can cause you as much trouble as building problems.

Reviewing the situation: two contrasting examples

The introduction of this book identified four 'types' of lessee-owned company. These, it must be emphasised, are not an exhaustive list but rather a way of demonstrating the potential versatility and variety of such organisations. Yours may not fit any one of them exactly, but they provide a set of models from which examples can be drawn demonstrating important points concerning the management of resident-owned companies.

The case for developing a management committee that fits your needs can be made by comparing and contrasting two 'types' of lessee-owned block with very different features, history, location and occupancy. In this case we compare a Type A and a Type C.

Type A

This example is a resident-owned company in Central London, with twenty flats. The building was bought in fairly good decorative condition but needs some attention. Amenities and services include twenty-four-hour porterage, satellite TV and passenger lift.

- **Reasons for purchase.** To raise standards, to control the abuse of leases and difficult tenants and to get good value for money on contracts. The landlord was willing to sell.

- **Residents.** They are older, professional and settled. The entrance decor is upmarket, with marble floor, curtains and tiebacks at the windows, polished hardwood, brass door furniture, leather seats and porter's desk. It has only a sixty-five per cent shareholder take-up among the lessees, some of whom are resident abroad. The company had to secure a bank loan to make up for this shortfall in take-up, and this is serviced out of ground rent income.

- **Management.** There is a group of experienced executives on the board for whom their London flat is mainly a weekday home. They instruct a West End firm of surveyors as managing agents and hold quarterly directors' meetings with them. Solicitors have been appointed to deal with the abuses of leases. Non-resident shareholder lessees increasingly want a say in the management of their block.

A comparison between the Type A company above and the following, a Type C, reveals a great deal about the influences that determine how each block decides to construct its main decision-making body, be it a board of directors or a wider based management committee.

Getting organised

Type C

This example is a resident-owned company in an unfashionable part of South East London. It runs a forty-flat building in which all but three of the flats are leased. The former landlord's interests were the rents on these three flats, their eventual sale value, a reasonably small ground rent on the rest, and a percentage mark-up on periodic redecorations contracts. Amenities and services include storage space for rent and a small rear garden.

- **Reasons for purchase.** It was a block where nothing seemed to get done, a situation which has resulted in a long list of outstanding jobs. Because inactivity was blamed on non-payment of service charges, the lessees wanted to control leasehold/freehold matters and the consequent erratic maintenance expenditure. Lastly they wanted to control contracts in order to raise standards and get better value for money.

- **Residents.** These are mainly young professionals (teachers, social workers, local government officers and civil servants) mostly on moderate incomes and therefore cost conscious. There are some families and also some difficult tenants. In every instance this is their only home. The entrance decor is painted woodwork and walls; stair nosings and lino treads. There is a door entry system and letter basket. It has no pretensions.

- **Management.** The property is managed by the lessee-owned company on a management committee basis, allocating roles and responsibilities to each of the committee members. It meets monthly and has no managing agent. Advice, when needed, is taken from a local firm of surveyors which has provided a surveyor's report on the whole premises. The management committee has used the report to set objectives to be met over a three-year period.

Both of the above resident companies have chosen a form of management to direct and control different sets of circumstances. These reflect the financial resources, the objectives and general style of each, but most of all, the inclination of each group of active residents to get personally involved and operate a hands-on approach to the property.

Type A, because of its maintenance record, may need less constant attention, but it cannot be neglected. Managing from a distance does not decrease the overall managerial responsibility of the directors for what has been bought. The appointed managing agent must therefore be an active and attentive participant in the management process. Regardless of the property, all resident-owned companies with lessee/shareholders need to know they are getting value for money.

> The Type C company has fewer resources, less experience of executive decision-making, fewer professional contacts, probably much more work to get through, many more problems of a domestic nature to address and, therefore, necessarily more personal enthusiasm for getting involved. The participants have chosen to set up a management committee meeting as frequently as required which reports to the board of the company. It would derive enthusiasm from those who are keen to be personally involved and on this basis build up expertise to meet objectives.
>
> One of the strongest influences determining the type of management organisation a lessee-owned company will choose is the recent history of the block. In Type C the management committee is taking a 'hands-on' approach in response to previous frustrations. On the other hand, very large blocks often like to keep their old tenants' associations running alongside the new company. Even though large numbers of flat-owners have come together and cooperated on the purchase of the freehold, perhaps creating close working relationships among a small group, the size and design of the building may still influence the nature of impersonal relationships where, for example, turnover in occupancy in rented flats has little bearing on flat-ownership and therefore lessee/shareholders.
>
> Moreover, where a small group may have been instrumental in organising the purchase and getting support for it throughout the block, there are always those who will assume that certain lessees promoted themselves on to the new management committee because of some ulterior motive or personal interest. Under such circumstances, and especially in the early days, an independent and continuing tenants' association can be a considerable benefit, taking some of the time-consuming tasks off the directors as well as assuring its members that there are checks on the activities of directors. It could also provide a member, or at least an observer, on the management committee.

If you want a substantial organisation on your side as you set out on the novel task of managing a block of flats, a tailor-made one exists. The Federation of Private Residents' Associations (FPRA) is a well-established membership organisation with over five hundred members. It has a comprehensive information pack and is able to give advice to members over a wide range of matters affecting resident-owned companies. For example, it will offer legal and practical advice on the extension and variation of leases. Its website is *www.fpra.org.uk*

Getting organised

ACTION

- Make a list of your own reasons for wanting to manage the building.
- With the other active members, draw up a second list representing what you all agree upon.
- Are there any differences in the two lists? If so, why?
- Compare results, and where there are substantial differences of opinion, address them and come to a working agreement. The most available starting place as an arbiter of purpose is the Memorandum of Association of the company (see Chapter 3), or Rules of the Society, if you are an Industrial and Provident Society. Usually people will be largely in agreement, in which case this exercise serves to focus on priorities and is a good basis for the beginnings of a working relationship.
- Write down your conclusions and keep them. They will almost certainly be needed in the future.

REFERENCE

The Federation of Private Residents' Associations, Enterprise House, 113–115 George Lane, South Woodford, London E18 1AB. Tel: 0208 530 8486. Website: *www.fpra.org.uk*

CHAPTER 2

Right to Manage companies

Right to Manage companies (referred to as RTM companies) are companies *limited by guarantee* and set up by no less than fifty per cent of the lessees of a residential property under the terms of the Commonhold and Leasehold Reform Act 2002 (referred to as CLRA). Their constitution is different from other types of resident-owned management companies referred to in this book. They exist to manage the property, not to own it. This chapter is about the managerial consequences of those rights and duties peculiar to RTM companies.

The subject of this book concerns the management of flats by their residents in whatever form they have established that function. So in the case of RTM companies, that would normally be from the *date of acquisition*, in other words, when the company becomes managerially responsible for the property. However, during the three months, or more, between the time the RTM company issued the formal *Notice of Claim* on the landlord and the day, not less than three months later, when it takes over the management, there are a number of administrative matters peculiar to this process, which have to be gone through. So this is a good time to double-check that each has been successfully completed so as to make the first days and months of the business of managing the premises as smooth as possible.

The first part of this chapter, therefore, considers some of the problems and opportunities that present themselves in the time running up to the acquisition date. The second part of the chapter will address more directly the managerial consequences peculiar to running a RTM company. To avoid unnecessary repetition, and where it is applicable to RTM companies, other chapters in this book will be referred to.

The new relationship between the RTM and landlord

A formal relationship between the *landlord*, who remains the *freeholder*, and the *leaseholders* continues, but on a significantly different basis than before. From now on the RTM company and the landlord deal directly with each other on all management matters. The right to set up a RTM company is a 'no-fault-based' right, which means that the law does not attribute blame to any of the parties involved. It is therefore possible that the handover of the management of the block has been a friendly and businesslike affair and that the landlord has been a willing party to the transfer. Other RTM companies will have been set up, in part, as the result of a long and bitter difference between the landlord and leaseholders. In either case, and in the event of any set of circumstances between those two extremes, it is in the interests of the RTM company to maintain a 'no fault' attitude and promote a professional and businesslike relationship with the landlord. Indeed, many landlords will be very happy to cooperate. Experience has shown that most resident companies return the building to a much better condition than when the landlord managed, and this can only be in his best interests, eventually reflected in the rents he is able to charge.

There are a number of areas where cooperation between the landlord and the RTM company will be most needed. These are as follows.

- **Where the landlord exercises his right to be a member of the RTM company.**

    Most landlords, friendly or otherwise, will almost certainly want to protect their investment in the property and, therefore, will want to join the company and exercise their voting rights. The landlord is entitled to be a member of the RTM company and will have a vote for each of the units he owns, either business or flats. If he does not own any units he is entitled to one vote as the freeholder. If the freeholder has let the whole property to someone (a **head lessee**) from whom you hold your leases (your landlord), then he is also entitled to vote by the same formula. Since most businesses work best when its members get on, this is a good opportunity to begin to develop good relations with the landlord – because he will always be there.

- **Where the RTM company is required by the landlord to collect the annual ground rent.**

    The lease requires leaseholders to pay an annual **ground rent** to the landlord. The landlord can require the RTM company to collect ground rent for him. This is not the **service charge**, which becomes the responsibility of the RTM company.

- **Where the RTM company needs the landlord to institute forfeiture proceedings for breaches of covenants by lessees.**

    The ultimate sanction the RTM company has over a lessee who is in constant breach of their lessee is *forfeiture*. But CLRA does not transfer this to the RTM company: it has to ask the landlord to process this through his solicitors. The whole question of forfeiture is a contentious one and is discussed at the end of this chapter.

- **Where the RTM company is required to keep the landlord informed.**
  The RTM company is given the power to issue **approvals** to flat-owners where the lease requires it. Examples include permission to make structural alterations to a flat, assigning a lease to another lessee and subletting. The RTM company must give either thirty or fourteen days' notice to the landlord before issuing approvals, depending upon the type of approval required.

A checklist prior to 'acquisition'

Having served the Notice of Claim on the landlord and set an acquisition date, there are a number of reasons why he in turn can serve a counter-notice to prevent you succeeding. You have obviously been through these hoops already but check them again in turn to avoid having to respond to a counter-notice which would require an application to the *Leasehold Valuation Tribunal* (LVT), which at this stage would be tedious and very distracting. Added to which the law can require you to pay the landlord's reasonable legal costs for issuing the counter-notice.

There are clear and detailed legal requirements here which are best carried out with the help of a legal adviser who specialises in property. Even though guidance is readily available, making the whole process fairly simple to follow, it is not advisable to take the whole thing on without professional help. There will be quite a lot of communicating for you to do among the leaseholders without having to worry about whether or not you have got all the legal requirements right. These are clearly presented in *The Right to Manage* booklet published by the *Leasehold Advisory Service* (LEASE). In particular, with your solicitor, satisfy yourself that both the substance and procedures required in setting up the RTM company have been completed correctly.

Check the information you need to help you manage

A management team needs resources, in this case, information and money. The second stage of information gathering will need your input. Prior to the acquisition date you are entitled to write to the landlord and receive within twenty-eight days, information you require in order to manage the property. The landlord is not required to cooperate in producing a definitive list; it is up to you to ask the right questions. And be sure to ask for this information more than twenty-eight days before the acquisition date so that it arrives in good time. Your list of questions will probably seek information in some of the following areas:

- Schedules and apportioning of service charges accounts.
- Copies of existing maintenance contracts, eg heating, building maintenance, lifts, pest control.
- Any surveyors' or other professional reports on the building.
- The most recent refurbishment contract specification.
- Existing building insurance policy and claims made on it.
- Guarantees of work on the building from past contracts, eg dry rot eradication, structural repairs, rising damp.
- Plans of the building, including drain plans.
- Copies of the lease (if not available).
- Schedule of current year's expenditure to date.
- Plans of alterations to flats and copies of permission given.
- Letting agreements and waiting lists – in the event that the RTM company is taking over the allocation of car parking and storage.
- Correspondence with statutory authorities relating to services.
- Any other administrative item peculiar to the idiosyncrasies of the property.

Service charges held by the landlord

The landlord, or his agent, must pay to the RTM company, on the date of acquisition or as soon as possible thereafter, all service charge monies they hold from the lessees. This will *exclude* the amount that the landlord can show that he needs in order to meet expenses for the property that he incurred *before* the acquisition date. If a figure cannot be agreed between the parties, the matter is referred to the Leasehold Valuation Tribunal. LEASE suggests that in all cases it would be sensible to appoint an external auditor to audit the service charge accounts, including, of course, any sinking fund monies that are held in trust by the landlord. If this is not immediately possible, and because you will need funds to start the business, agree a lower figure 'without prejudice' to further payments which you will request and await the decision of the Tribunal, which may take some time.

By the same token, unpaid service charges that were owed to the landlord prior to the acquisition date must still be paid to him. If there are any individual service charge payments outstanding, it would be good practice to encourage every leaseholder who joins the company to clear their debts to the landlord. While he may still have to pursue non-paying non-members, the RTM company has shown good faith in helping to progress the handover.

Deciding what to do about the landlord's existing contracts

This is a thorny problem because in law, all the landlord's contracts with his contractors who service the property, cease on the date of acquisition. It is likely that there will be in existence a number of contracts between the landlord, or his agent, and various contractors for services that are being provided to the property. These may cover general maintenance, gardening, cleaning, lift maintenance, managing agent and caretaker/porterage. The last we can deal with separately.

The legal position

When the landlord received your initial Notice of Claim stating your intentions to become a RTM company, he was obliged to inform all those with whom he had contracts relating to the management of the property, that those contracts would end. They in turn should have done the same to their subcontractors. However, you may wish to retain the services of some contractors and rid yourselves of others. The law, which will affect your decision about them, says two things:

- First, that on the acquisition date, ie the day when the RTM company takes over the management, all these contracts will be deemed in law to have been frustrated (that means ceased to exist or broken).

- Second, that when this happens, 'the ordinary law of contract will apply' and where this process frustrates a contract 'each party will have the right to recover moneys due to them from the other party' (Lord Falkner). In other words the RTM company could find itself at the end of a chain of claims for breach of contract between the landlord and those with whom he has had contracts.

So a prudent course of action for any new RTM company would be to show that you have behaved reasonably in circumstances over which you had no immediate control.

As early as possible within the three months before the date of acquisition obtain the details of all these contracts from the landlord or his agent. They are required in law to reply within twenty-eight days. To avoid the possibility of litigation, it may be sensible to give notice of your intention to take over all the existing contracts. Of those whose services you do not wish to retain, you can, in due course, invoke their determination clause (which is the agreed way, in a contract, of ending it). A good solicitor will guide you through this. So let each contractor know where they will stand with regard to the RTM company on the acquisition date.

Transfer of staff

Dealing with the employment contracts of existing staff, such as a resident caretaker, is somewhat clearer in law. To be precise, the Transfer of Undertakings (Protection of Employment) Regulations 1981 will probably enable a landlord's employee, such as a caretaker, to transfer employment directly to the RTM company without your consent on the same conditions as their existing employment (except pensions rights) thus avoiding redundancy. If he is good at his job and you want to retain his services, there is no problem. But, you may find yourself the new employer of a member of staff whom, for some years, you have found unsuitable and whose services you do not wish to retain. Your duty is to behave as a reasonable and responsible employer, and unless you have clear evidence that the employee is unsuitable for legal reasons (under which circumstances you would take advice on how to terminate the employment), wipe the slate clean and adopt the advice given in Chapter 12, 'Managing staff'. This may involve appointing a director to liaise directly with the employee, re-establishing a good working relationship based upon the contract of employment and reviewing performance at regular intervals. At all times be scrupulously fair within the terms of the contract of employment in dealing with any disciplinary matters which might lead to dismissal. The ACAS booklet *Employing People* is a good starting place as a source of information.

Understanding the scope of your new powers

The *Lease* and the *Memorandum and Articles of Association* are a good basis upon which to build your understanding of your formal responsibilities for managing the property. They both prescribe the scope of your managerial authority and responsibility and provide the opportunities and occasions to exercise them. These two sets of documents are formal legal documents which look a bit daunting at first sight, but in fact are easily understood.

The Lease

Chapter 6 contains an introduction to reading a lease and that is a useful starting point in order to understand the structure of a lease. Its purpose is to help you find your way around the various parts of a lease and explains where to locate the landlord's and leaseholder's covenants (obligations) within it.

The Memorandum and Articles of Association

The Memorandum and Articles of Association are in fact two documents, always found together. The heading of each states that yours is 'a company limited by guarantee and not having a share capital' (see Chapter 3, 'Limited liability').

Generally speaking, the Memorandum of Association says what the company has been set up to do and the Articles of Association say how it must do it. They are often referred to as the **'Mem and Arts'** and yours will probably be held by your company secretary. Because there is a special format for RTM companies it is possible to access a standard copy of a RTM company's Mem and Arts from the HMSO website so you can print it off for you own purposes (*www.hmso.gov.uk* – look for Statutory Instrument 2003 No 2120). They have been skilfully written to help the RTM company to conduct its business with clauses sometimes allowing for hiccups that may occur along the way, stressing the benefit of good intention and best interest of the company, rather than requiring adherence to the strictest rules that could prevent things getting done (eg see Section 78 of the Articles of Association). Nonetheless, the law requires you to conduct business as a well-run company and make every effort to adhere to the rights and duties set down in them.

Memorandum of Association of an RTM company

Sections 1, 2 and 3 of the Memorandum are short. They contain the name of the company, where it is registered, identifying your premises by name and stating the company's purpose – which is to manage it. Section 4 gives the RTM company the 'power to do all such things as may be authorised or required to be done by a RTM company by and under the 2002 Act'. It then, without detracting from the general objective above, cites twenty-six sections (a–z) identifying your company's particular rights and duties. They cover items involving the right to manage the property, grant approvals, relations with landlord, variation of leases, maintenance, contracts, litigation, insurance, service charges, trusts, sinking funds, lending and borrowing, bank accounts, pensions and gratuities, determining voting and other rights from building measurements, agreements with central or local government, adherence to the Articles of Association and, finally, pursuing the interests of the company anywhere, lawfully.

Three short sections complete the Memorandum. Section 7 describes the financial commitment of members in the event of the company ceasing to exist. Section 8 says what happens to any surplus cash in that event. Section 9 reminds you that as the laws of the land cited in the Memorandum of Association change, so do your obligations.

Articles of Association of an RTM company

The Articles of Association, which say how the company is to be run, are longer and more detailed but are tailor-made for RTM companies. They are essential reading and, with a little assistance and a pencil to underline sections of note along the way, can be understood quite easily. They follow the format of a normal document of this kind and have separate, and sometimes detailed, sections on members, meetings, directors, minutes, rights of inspection and copying of company books and records, the issuing of notices, directors' indemnity and finally, a short section on 'Rules or By-Laws'. This last section allows the directors 'from time to time [to] make such rules or by-laws as they may deem necessary or expedient or convenient for the proper conduct and management of the Company'.

The important proviso to this is that new rules (see Appendix 3, 'House Rules') must be consistent with the Memorandum and Articles of Association. So the powers that are given in these documents are both general, enabling the company to run itself with some latitude, and specific, with matters being highlighted which require special attention. In times of uncertainty the Mem and Arts is one of your points of secure reference. It helps enormously to know your way around it especially when you are being pressed by a lessee to do something that is not included in the Mem and Arts and is therefore beyond the competence of the company.

Managing the property

On the date of acquisition, the RTM company takes over the broad range of managerial duties which, in your residential leases, are described as the landlord's. These include:

- The supply of services
- Repairs to the fabric
- General maintenance
- Improvements to the property
- Building insurance
- Management of staff.

These areas of responsibility are discussed under the other chapter headings in this book with specific advice and guidance with further references and checklists for action. Except where this chapter is specific (eg relations with the landlord) the content of these other chapters applies equally to a residential property managed by an RTM company.

Responsibilities not transferred to the RTM company

Some landlord responsibilities are not included. Your own lease is emphasised here as a guide to your own responsibilities because the management of *non-residential* parts of the building is not transferred to you. Neither (except for structural repairs) is the responsibility for the management of the flats the landlord continues to own. The first of these exceptions presents a problem which needs addressing.

- **Non-residential parts** of the building remain the responsibility of the landlord. This creates a potential source of conflict where you will get no help from CLRA. So, if you can, and as early as possible, identify with the landlord areas of potential conflict between the residential and non-residential parts of the property. In other words, those parts which the RTM company manages and those for which the landlord continues to be responsible. The interests of the residential part of the building and thus the RTM company, may not be the same as those of the landlord and the non-residential parts. For example, conflicts of interest may arise where flats, shops and offices are adjacent to one another and share services or common parts.

  The point here is that there is no provision in law for the resolution of differences where residential and non-residential interests conflict and if you can't negotiate your way out of a problem, the alternative is arbitration or going to court. So agree a 'prenuptial' conflict agreement, for example one which identifies areas where the interest of one side or the other is given preference, or, as a last resort, both sides agree to accept a nominated local surveyor's or arbitrator's decision, at reasonable cost. This can help avoid long and expensive disputes later on. It may even be necessary to call in a third party to help mediate the formation of such an agreement. The emphasis here is on the importance and value of cooperation between the parties before the actual conflicts arise.

- **Flats the landlord owns** remain his to let and determine what happens in them, in accordance with the lease.
- **Forfeiture** is the ultimate sanction a landlord has in order to enforce the terms of the lease when a lessee is in continuous breach of its covenants. This power is not transferred and remains the landlord's. In order to back its authority as the managing company, the RTM company is required in law to seek the cooperation of the landlord.

Forfeiture and repossession

This subject is contentious. On the one hand it is seen to be unfair because a flat-owner could lose a property he has paid for, and on the other necessary, because it is the effective sanction that can be used by a landlord against a leaseholder who continues to ignore the terms of his lease. It is called *forfeiture*. It requires the landlord, within the terms of the lease, through his solicitor, to issue a Section 146 Notice. Unlike all of the other **rights and duties** of the landlord in law, this one has not been transferred to the RTM company, but remains the right of the landlord – who no longer manages the property.

> *The procedure*
>
> On the occasions the RTM company needs to deal with a lessee who has been repeatedly in breach of their lease and refuses to change whatever it is that is causing the problem, a rather cumbersome provision in law requires the company to ask the landlord to ask his solicitor to initiate proceedings to issue the Section 146 Notice. Added to which, the law now requires the landlord to prove the breach of covenant or the service charge debt before serving a Section 146 Notice. This has to be proven before the Leasehold Valuation Tribunal.
>
> The landlord must first obtain an admission from the leaseholder that he is in breach of the lease, or that the service charge payments are in arrears. If the leaseholder for any reason does not agree, the landlord must apply to the Leasehold Valuation Tribunal so that it can determine that an unresolved breach of lease has occurred or that the arrears of service charge exist, are reasonable and must be paid.

> In the case of arrears of service charge, the leaseholder can challenge the reasonableness of the service charge. Therefore, he may admit that he is in arrears but require the Leasehold Valuation Tribunal to state that the unpaid charge was reasonable (remembering, of course, that those who set the service charge have probably already paid it). At the tribunal hearing, the landlord must produce evidence, obviously provided by the company, to substantiate the reasonableness of the service charge demand. This may include the appropriate paperwork, estimates, accounts, service agreements, minutes of meetings, competitive tenders and interim notices on works carried out and final invoices etc.
>
> In the case of unpaid service charge, the Leasehold Valuation Tribunal must state both that the leaseholder is in arrears, and how much he owes the company. The leaseholder has fourteen days from the date of the Leasehold Valuation Tribunal's decision to rectify the breach of lease or to pay the debt before the landlord can serve a Section 146 Notice for forfeiture. The Tribunal does not consider sums of £350 or less, unless they have been outstanding for three years (application to the Small Claims Court would recover these).

Because neither the leaseholder nor the landlord has any immediate interest in settling the matter – the leaseholder not wanting to pay or rectify the problem, the landlord neither receiving any service charge nor living on the premises – it would seem good managerial sense for the RTM company to administer as much of this as they are able before handing it over to the landlord to issue the Section 146 Notice. If the objecting leaseholder decides to respond to the RTM company, and not insist that he will only deal lawfully with the landlord, it may be possible to obtain agreement from the leaseholder that the debt or the breach of lease exists.

The only legitimate interest the RTM company can have under these circumstances is the recovery of service charges. However, one possible interest the landlord might show in the legal process is the likelihood of forfeiture of the lease and his repossession of the flat. A landlord may approach you, where a defaulting leaseholder was particularly disorganised, to come to an 'arrangement' with him concerning the conduct of the case – which would give you an interesting problem, requiring a balance of conscience against duty of care to the company. You will always need to deal with the landlord and in some circumstances you will need a long spoon.

It is good practice, even under these trying circumstances, to be seen to be doing everything both correctly and quickly. The RTM company is usually looking for an early resolution to the problem, not the repossession of a flat. Swift managerial action impresses upon the leaseholder that your intentions are lawful and informed, which may result in an early resolution if, in fact, he privately recognises the reasonableness of your case. Added to which it will demonstrate to other leaseholders who abide by the terms of their lease and pay their service charges, that you have dealt as efficiently as you can with the problem.

Until recently, the lawful, considered and reasonable threat of a Section 146 Notice, without even issuing one, could be sufficient to settle a problem that a resident-owned company might have had with an irresponsible lessee. Regrettably, there has been a record of private landlords abusing the threat of forfeiture, which is why the law is now designed to protect the innocent lessee, giving the responsible RTM company a much weaker hand in managing difficult cases of breach of lease. The law thus places leaseholders who take over the management of their blocks in a catch-22. On the one hand they want to manage their own block because it is so badly managed at present, and on the other, the law now binds them to the inclinations of the same landlord who instructed the type of management they are attempting to dispose of.

Although its ultimate effect was designed to return the ownership of a lease and therefore the flat, back to the landlord, it seldom did. This is because it required the consent of a court of law and experience shows that judges do not turn people out of their homes on to the streets. Even so it was abused in that form. It has been suggested, therefore, that forfeiture should be abolished because it has been known to end in repossession.

But an RTM company needs the authority to manage its responsibility effectively. Three points in defence of retaining a realistic management sanction for non-payment of service charges and continuous breaches of lease can be made here:

- First, it is most likely that every flat-dweller is going to suffer from continued abuse by a neighbour in an adjacent flat at some time or another. Certainly, those who have had to put up with the continued bad behaviour of neighbours and who themselves keep the terms of their lease, would want to know that an effective sanction against blatant breach of lease is available.

- Second, the recent increase in numbers of 'buy to let' flats in residential blocks has produced a substantial 'renting subtenant' population. Where an absentee investor is looking to make continuous income from the flat, a succession of subtenants may pass through the building who know nothing of the lease, use the rented flat as a base for parties or a caravanserai for friends, to the constant nightmare of neighbouring owner-occupiers. The absentee flat-owner is not aware of this, neither does he care because he does not live there. He is very happy just letting his flat through an agent and receiving his rent every month. Experience has shown that the ability in law to issue the threat of a Section 146 Notice has returned life in a 'nightmare property' to peace and tranquillity.

- Third, in twenty-five years' experience of managing residential properties, wholly owned by resident companies, a Section 146 Notice has hardly ever been issued irresponsibly by a resident-owned company.

In managerial terms, the threat of forfeiture (or perhaps a more workable replacement) has a proper function. This has just as much to do with the management of the property as the ownership of it. Its purpose here is to ensure that those who have the responsibility of managing the property have the ability to apply the lease where it is being abused. If a subtenant of an absentee leaseholder is causing a complete nuisance, and if he decides he is not going to cooperate with the RTM company's request to stop, the management company must, in all cases, be able to act with authority to resolve the problem. Furthermore, when the resolution of a dispute between two or more leaseholders rests on the responsibility of the RTM company to apply ***mutual enforceability of covenants*** in the lease (see Chapter 6), it must be able to show that it can back its authority to resolve such a dispute. So it not only needs an effective sanction in order to exercise its responsibilities, it also needs control over that sanction. At present, the law does not provide this without the active cooperation of the landlord.

So a further necessary question remains: What is an RTM company to do when it is the subtenant of a landlord's rented flat who is causing the problem? He has received a series of reminders from the company about, shall we say, excessive multiple occupancy or continuous noisy late-night parties, and as a consequence the landlord is required by the RTM company to take action against himself. The threat becomes risible. He is unlikely to do it if it will disrupt his letting and lose him rental income. Apart from which, to whom would he forfeit the lease on his own flat? So there is a further case for promoting a good working relationship with the landlord, not to mention a more workable replacement to forfeiture.

Approvals

The RTM company has the power to issue *approvals* required by the lease, with the proviso that it gives the landlord due notice. Residential leases usually require flat-owners to seek approval for a number of things they might wish to do. Examples are the intention to make structural alterations to a flat, to sublet it or alter the services to it. Different leases contain different items requiring approvals so yours may contain some and not others. While the RTM company will issue the approval, it must give thirty days' notice to the landlord for the following approval requests:

- Assigning the lease to another purchaser (ie selling the flat)
- Subletting the flat, or part of it, to a tenant
- Placing a charge on the flat (ie raising a loan or obtaining a mortgage on it)
- Parting with possession
- Altering the flat structurally (removing or adding walls)
- Making improvements to the flat (eg adding a bathroom)
- Changing the use of the flat (eg using it primarily as an office).

Apart from the above, fourteen days is the standard length of notice you must give the landlord for other approvals you have been asked to grant by a flat-owner.

The landlord may reply in one of three ways. He may agree, so if you wish, you can simply go ahead and issue the approval. He may ignore you, in which case you can issue the approval anyway because if he doesn't reply you do not need his active support. Or he may, for his own reasons, object. In which case, if you can, try the conflict resolution route in order to get agreement. Because the alternative involves an application to the Leasehold Valuation Tribunal, an exchange of paperwork and a great deal of time and effort preparing and explaining a case to an official body, probably involving a potential subtenant into the bargain, in the hope that your view will prevail.

There is, of course, the other alternative, namely, that the landlord persuades you of the sense of his case and you then see good reason to refuse to give the approval. It is possible that in granting an approval you might be creating a problem for one of his non-residential units, which would be a fair reason for accepting his objection.

However, when issuing an approval, you would only do so making sure the leaseholder receiving it conforms to all the statutory and other requirements that apply in that case (see Appendix 2A, 'Building works and the refurbishment of flats'). This should not create a problem for you. The lease will almost certainly require the recipient of the approval to pay the RMT company's reasonable professional costs in appointing a surveyor or solicitor to represent and advise you or act for you in ensuring that the work or transaction is carried out properly. This is an example where the appointment of, and working with, a good professional is essential (see Chapter 5).

ACTION

Prior to the acquisition date

- Check that the landlord cannot object to the setting up of the RTM company at the last minute.
- Make a list of all the administrative information you will need from the landlord to set up and run the management company.
- Decide what to do about the landlord's 'frustrated' contracts.
- Try to agree a method of resolving potential conflicts with the landlord.
- Study your own lease. It will usually be the same as every other leaseholder's in the building.
- Read the Mem and Arts of the new RTM company.

REFERENCES

Obtain a copy of your Memorandum and Articles of Association. (A model of this can be printed off from the HMSO website, *www.hmso.gov.uk*: you need Statutory Instrument 2003 No 2120.)

If you have not already got it, obtain a copy of *The Right to Manage* booklet published by the Leasehold Advisory Service. Tel: 0845 345 1993. Website: *www.lease-advice.org*

Employing People, published by the Advisory, Conciliation and Arbitration Service (ACAS) – *www.acas.org.uk* – is a beginner's book, is well presented and gives further simple but authoritative references.

CHAPTER 3

The company, its directors and their duties

Whichever route you have taken to incorporation, you should now have a properly constituted company under company law. As an RTM or RTE company the process will be complete. If you are a freehold buyout, the company may still be in a transitional stage, having so far been operated by a small group of residents on behalf of the remainder. If the company was bought 'off the shelf', its Memorandum and Articles of Association (see below) may not be as well drafted as you would want. There may be particular features relating to the building itself – its recent history, its locality or the residential make-up of its occupants – that warrant special clauses in the Memorandum and Articles of Association about your objects and purpose as a company: concerning, for example, voting rights or officers. In fact, it is now possible to purchase an off-the-shelf company that is suitable for lessee-owned companies and which may, with modest alterations, be tailored to your purposes.

Alternative structures of accountability

There are a number of alternative approaches to setting up the decision-making body that will manage the property on a day-to-day basis. As has already been discussed, organisation Types A and B (running larger or more upmarket blocks) will probably use the *board of directors* as the sole decision-making body and appoint a managing agent to carry out the day-to-day management. Types C and D (less affluent or smaller organisations) will want a more versatile managing body with an active and involved membership able to carry out projects and meet as required in sub-committees or interest groups, reporting regularly to a *management committee*. This committee will have been set up by, and will report to, the board of directors.

In both cases the centre of authority is the board of directors of the company. The Type C and D management committee structures will be discussed in the next chapter. The reason for discussing the company here is that it has a central legal and decision-making role which must be understood. In so far as it is relevant to Types A and B, the board's potential as a managing body will also be discussed.

Information from Companies House for smaller companies

Companies House has issued a helpful document (*Flat Management Companies*, GBA9) which applies specifically to companies run for the benefit of lessees rather than to those being run as a business or for profit. On the face of it, the statutory requirements that apply to running a company seem to be both arduous and unnecessary, especially if you are a very small company. This now need not be so and the helpful innovations that will benefit small companies can be listed as follows.

- Small companies with only a few bills for, say, repairs and maintenance, may adopt some less formal way of dealing with them, so that the company itself may be allowed to become 'dormant' (see Companies House booklet GBA10). In that case all that would be required would be a simple balance sheet which would *not* have to be audited. However, this would still have to be shown to shareholders and sent to the Registrar of Companies.

- Shareholders of a company may pass a resolution to the effect that they do not wish to hold Annual General Meetings in the future. A copy of this resolution must be sent to the Registrar of Companies.

- Small companies may prepare accounts for their members under the special provisions of Section 246 and 246A of the Companies Act 1985. In addition, they may prepare and deliver abbreviated accounts to the Registrar (see Companies House booklet GBA3 for details of the exemptions). Small companies can be exempted from the need to have the accounts audited. However, except in the case of dormant accounts, the shareholders or the directors may wish to have an audit to ensure that flat-owners can see that everything is 'above board'.

- The annual return to Companies House is no longer tied to the date of the Annual General Meeting. But it must be delivered to the Registrar of Companies within twenty-eight days of the date to which it is made up – with the filing fee.

The benefits of these provisions go a long way towards appeasing the frequent and fair complaint that the statutory costs of auditing and associated fees are prohibitive for the smaller company. Lessees are said to feel more secure in the knowledge that the landlord's functions are being fulfilled by a lessee-owned body incorporated under company law, and that those who are acting on their behalf are required to conduct business and themselves in accordance with legally enforceable directors' duties. In smaller companies, the benefits have often seemed marginal when statutory fees have to be paid. Now this need not be so.

The company

The company is a legal entity. It can for example sue, or be sued by, any of its members, the shareholders. The company, being the owner of the freehold title, is the lessor and landlord and therefore carries full legal responsibility for the property.

Legal documents

There are four important documents that are specific to your company:

- The **Certificate of Incorporation**, which *identifies* it.
- The **Memorandum**, which states *what it has been set up to do*.
- The **Articles of Association**, which describe *how it must function as a company*.
- The **Land Certificate**, which proves that the company owns the property.

The Certificate of Incorporation

The Certificate of Incorporation may be regarded as the company's birth certificate. It will have been issued by the Registrar of Companies and states its name and the date the company was set up. If you so wish, there is a simple procedure for changing its name. This document may be required as evidence that the company is what it claims to be, for example if it is seeking a loan from a bank or when it has to identify itself for legal purposes.

The Memorandum of Association

The Memorandum of Association is a fairly short and easily read document. It can be likened to the company's 'job description'. It states what the company has been set up to do, what its overall aims are and what is special about it. The company will not normally enter into any activity that is outside of the stated areas of the Memorandum of Association; indeed, it is *legally bound* to act within its terms. You should obtain your own personal copy from your company secretary.

The Articles of Association

The Articles of Association may be seen as the company's 'internal rules'. These say how the company is to be run. They lay down who is allowed to hold shares, who can be a director, who may be an officer, and how long these posts can be held, how voting will be conducted and other details which state how the company is to carry out its business. Again, this is a short, self-explanatory document which will reward a few quiet moments' careful reading.

The Memorandum of Association and the Articles of Association are often referred to together as the *'Mem and Arts'*.

This is a good time to get a copy of all three documents and become familiar with them, so that any early misunderstandings about the company, its lawful purposes and the manner in which it is to conduct itself can be properly discussed. If necessary, professional advice should be taken so that the matter can be sorted out to best effect.

Amendments to the Memorandum and Articles of Association

If your company has been bought off-the-shelf, you may well wish to tailor the Memorandum and Articles of Association to suit the particular needs of your block. Such amendments require the agreement of a seventy-five per cent majority of shareholders. Lessee-owned companies are often set up by a small delegation of perhaps two or three individuals, representing all participating leaseholders and acting on the advice of a professional. They are often advised to get their Memorandums and Articles of Association sorted out properly *before* shares are actually issued among the lessees, simply to avoid the time-consuming and sometimes problematic process of securing a formal seventy-five per cent agreement.

It is worth remembering that if a requirement is put into the Memorandum rather than the Articles of Association, and if the Memorandum prohibits any alteration to itself, then the requirement becomes ***unalterable in law***. In this way shareholders can be limited permanently to lessees and directors to shareholders. This can prevent anyone who has not got a direct financial stake in the property and who will not be a service charge payer exercising control within the company and will keep at a respectable distance overprotective family solicitors and doting godsons with an eye to the main chance.

But times change, and needs change with them, so what is considered a desirable rule now and something worth enshrining in the Memorandum of Association for the lifetime of the company, may well be a burden to future generations of directors.

Company rules and non-members

Company rules only apply to those who belong to the company, and some of the lessees might not be members. It is thus not possible to require such a lessee to abide by the company's rules. In this instance it is always the lease that determines the relationship between lessor (the company) and lessee. (Chapter 10 examines and develops these points further.) It follows that new lessees cannot be required to join the company and become shareholders. People must do so willingly – and they will, if the incentives are sufficiently attractive. One major attraction is the offer of a longer and better lease, which is frequently the principal reason why lessees buy their blocks of flats in the first place. This will be discussed in Chapter 6, together with examples and improvements that can become part of a new lease.

Limited liability

The company is called a *limited* company because those who support it financially, its members, do so only to a limited extent. A limited company can be limited in one of two ways:

- **By guarantee**, which means that each member has made an undertaking to finance the company's losses to a fixed sum of money.

  If your company is limited by guarantee it can have, in theory, any number of members and the irksome process of the transfer of shares every time a flat is sold becomes unnecessary. If the Memorandum and Articles so instruct, the outgoing lessee loses his right to membership and the incoming one becomes a member, accepting his predecessor's liability which is usually fixed at £1.

- **By shares,** which means that the shareholders have bought shares in the company with money the company now holds, and they cannot be required to pay more. Lessee-owned companies do not trade in the normal commercial sense and their shares are allocated usually for nominal sums of money. They would therefore only become insolvent as a result of severe neglect, stupidity or an illegal act.

  If your company is limited by shares, check the Articles of Association to see how they are allocated. One per flat is usual and joint owners of a flat can be joint owners of the shares. But in some smaller lessee-owned properties the allocation of shares, and therefore voting rights, may for very good reasons favour, for example, a group of very large flats that pay proportionally more in service charge. This arrangement is, however, rare.

The initial share allocation might only be temporary, depending on the circumstances in which the company was established. A company that has bought a freehold with the financial support of, say, seventy-five per cent of lessees will have required each lessee to pay (a) their individual share of the purchase price, plus (b) a proportion of the outstanding twenty-five per cent of the total cost. The shareholding will adjust over a period of time as either (a) new lessees buy flats off non-participating lessees and join the scheme, or (b) non-participating lessees subsequently join. As new shareholders buy in, their contribution may be apportioned among the initial shareholders who carried the financial burden of the buyout.

The alternative method of financing a freehold purchase without full participation requires a bank loan to make up the difference between the amount contributed by the initial members and the full purchase price. Interest on the loan is paid from the ground rent received on those flats that remain owned by non-members of the company. As more flats eventually join, contributors pay off the principal of the loan until, ideally, all the flat-owners are shareholders. In this way the initial group of lessees who buy out the block does not carry the financial burden.

Note: throughout this book, for the sake of simplicity, the term 'shareholders' is used to describe members of both kinds of limited company.

Company assets

A lessee-owned company has few realisable assets – that is, money that is paid directly to the company and is not part of the service charge. These assets might include the ground rent and the rent from the caretaker's flat, if there is one; proceeds from the hire of garages and storage space perhaps; and the small amount guaranteed by shareholders, which seldom amounts to more than £1 per flat. For this reason, the company is unable to incur large company debts for which it cannot provide adequate collateral. All company financial undertakings should take this into account. The company would not, for example, attempt to fund a private property development activity with its assets.

This does not, of course, prevent the directors signing contracts for considerable amounts of money for redecoration and repairs under the lease. In these instances there is always reasonable expectation that adequate sums will be forthcoming from service charges, which themselves, by law, may only be spent on certain items (see Chapter 6). Large lessee-owned companies frequently enter into contracts for six-figure sums without any reason to doubt their capacity to pay for the works in full.

The company's main source of funds for necessary expenditure is the *service charge*, money they receive from lessees and hold in trust under the terms of the lease. It is therefore obvious that when lessees do not pay their service charge – either because they cannot afford to or because they are just being difficult – the company's cash flow can be adversely affected, often resulting in delays in getting projects done. Chapter 10 examines in greater detail the topic of difficult payers.

Corporate structure and accountability

The theory

The formal pattern as illustrated in **Figure 1** is as follows. A *company* is owned by its *shareholders* (in this case lessee/shareholders) who elect, normally from their number, the *board of directors*, who in turn elect their own *chairman*.

The directors are responsible for the management of the property and may either decide to manage the building themselves or delegate its day-to-day running either to a *managing agent* or to a *management committee* which it will appoint. The management committee may decide to delegate some of its work to *sub-committees*. On the face of it the whole thing is a comfortably accountable process with everybody who holds a position of authority being responsible ultimately to the shareholders.

This model continues as follows. The shareholders appoint *auditors* to formally check that the accounts are legal and correct. The audited accounts are presented to the shareholders at each *Annual General Meeting* (AGM). The shareholders at the AGM, or, where called, an *Extraordinary General Meeting* (EGM), have the authority to appoint and dismiss directors and auditors.

The reality

As you might expect, the reality can be very different from this. Often companies, and especially smaller ones – for example those we have already identified as Types B and D – may be run by groups of

How to manage your own block of flats

FIGURE 1 Model of company accountability

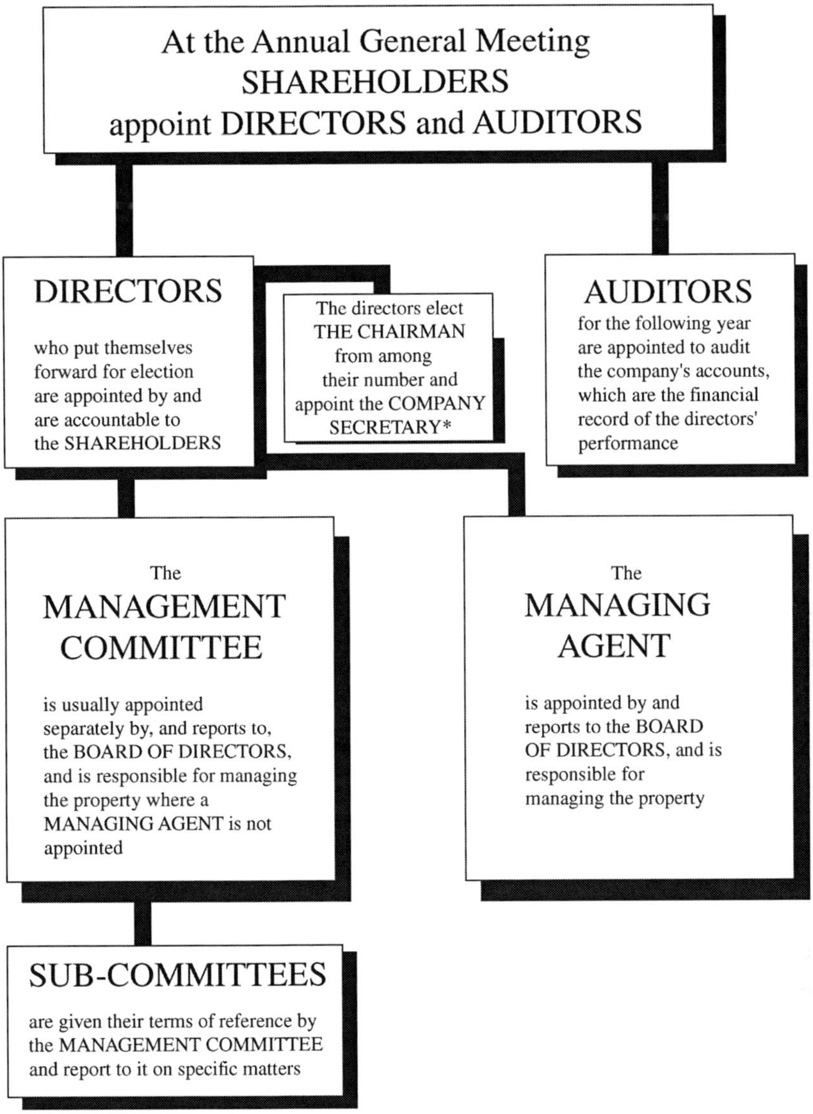

At the Annual General Meeting SHAREHOLDERS appoint DIRECTORS and AUDITORS

DIRECTORS

who put themselves forward for election are appointed by and are accountable to the SHAREHOLDERS

The directors elect THE CHAIRMAN from among their number and appoint the COMPANY SECRETARY*

AUDITORS

for the following year are appointed to audit the company's accounts, which are the financial record of the directors' performance

The MANAGEMENT COMMITTEE

is usually appointed separately by, and reports to, the BOARD OF DIRECTORS, and is responsible for managing the property where a MANAGING AGENT is not appointed

The MANAGING AGENT

is appointed by and reports to the BOARD OF DIRECTORS, and is responsible for managing the property

SUB-COMMITTEES

are given their terms of reference by the MANAGEMENT COMMITTEE and report to it on specific matters

*Company secretary: the directors may choose to appoint a professional to this post rather than a resident lessee.

knowledgeable businessmen, administrators or professionals. These are often retired people with time and interest who are broadly familiar with the legal requirements. They might meet monthly in a committee, which typically includes a group of willing helpers, who themselves eventually become valuable contributors.

If there is a managing agent he may attend the meetings or be instructed the next morning and asked to confirm his instructions and intended action in writing. If the directors are managing the building themselves, the appropriate responsible director will instruct whatever has to be done. He will ensure it is checked before payment is made and will report back to the committee. The committee will keep a controlling eye on the money and will report formally to lessee/shareholders at the AGM. When the block is running well, the business of the AGM is not always well attended. Often people seem to arrive towards the end when the bottles are being opened – meetings of successful lessee-owned companies can be very sociable events.

The directors are often known to a number of other residents and, far from being the focus of constant scrutiny, are initially seen as guardians of the peace and arbiters of good sense. As time goes by, interests naturally ebb and flow, and the block may go through periods of change and uncertainty. For instance, a new lessee who has not experienced the initial buyout may think that it is all too good to be true and may push for a change at the helm. Some directors may willingly hand over the reins and take a back seat while someone else has a go. It is then announced that everything appears to have been carried out very well and the misunderstanding seems to have arisen from a lack of communication. Few chairmen and directors, having successfully managed the building through the difficult early days and having achieved a measure of managerial stability for the new company, are foolish enough to abuse a position that is openly accountable to most of their neighbours.

This often repeated story provides a lesson: no matter how well the place is run or how little interest the shareholders seem to display in the business of the company, it is best to maintain open and frequent communication and obvious checks and balances, so that good is always seen to be done. Do not expect the organisation to run itself: manage the communications.

The first company meeting as landlord

The first formal meeting following the purchase of the property is important, as it will affect all those that follow. It must therefore make its decisions carefully and not be drawn into addressing questions that can wait for a more appropriate moment. The meeting should be held as soon as possible after the purchase, on an ad hoc agenda, to:

- Decide on the management structure
- Appoint a full board of directors
- Announce the financial position.

The group handling the affairs of the company during the buyout should circulate this brief agenda to all participating lessees, giving correct notice, time and place. There is no reason why the meeting should not discuss other items than the above, but the first objective should be to get the organisation up and running so that there is action to report to the next meeting.

Deciding on management structure

High on the agenda must be the form of management the company intends to adopt. The decision required can be described as follows. Should the company (a) appoint a managing agent, or (b) carry out the management functions itself?

If (a), who should be considered? If (b), should the board of directors manage directly, or should a management committee be appointed?

Appointing the full board of directors

In some companies the appointment of a full board of directors will have been delayed until this time, probably because the freehold purchase only requires a nominal director plus a company secretary for the company to exist and authorise the transaction.

The company is a legal entity and will be responsible, as defined by its Memorandum and Articles of Association, for the management of the block. Consequently the following appointments need to be made or confirmed in order to give the company direction:

1 Appointment of directors
2 Appointment of a chairman
3 Appointment/confirmation of the company secretary.

This order is important, because the shareholders appoint the directors, the directors appoint the chairman and the directors appoint the company secretary. But what is more significant at this stage, directors may co-opt new directors between AGMs. In this way, most boards of directors take shape in their first year of life.

1 The appointment of directors

In theory, a non-trading company such as a lessee-owned company can exist in law with just one director and a company secretary. In practice, there are a number of reasons why a board of directors is desirable:

- To provide a forum for debate
- To get a majority view to represent shareholders' views on important matters
- To provide continuity when directors resign and move away
- To provide impersonal corporate decisions when difficult personal matters are concerned, especially unpopular but necessary decisions.

As mentioned above, directors can usually be co-opted up to the permitted number at any directors' meeting between AGMs. Good practice at the outset is to appoint only as many as are immediately needed. There may be a number of people who want to serve and will allow their names to be put forward. A block with six staircases may decide that it is best represented by a director for each staircase. Another (for example a Type A block) may want its tenants' representatives to be separate from the board, acting as a tenants' watchdog committee.

Either way the company is responsible for a long enough list of things to provide appropriate responsibilities for a group of directors, although in smaller buildings individual directors will probably handle a number of different tasks. Broadly speaking, these are similar to the required and expected activities of the company and cover the things for which informed decisions must be made for the company to function effectively. The list of directors and roles might be as follows:

- Chairman and company secretary (statutory requirements)
- Finance (accounts, service charge demands and payment of invoices)
- Residents (communications)
- Staff (employment)
- Building (inspections, surveyor)
- Common parts and services (maintenance of)
- Amenities (allocation and maintenance of).

At this stage the number of directors appointed should be enough to cover the immediate needs. Each one usually develops an interest in their allocated area and becomes the block 'expert'. This then is their role – their required or expected behaviour – and identifies their responsibilities.

Although the company will by its very nature advance the interests of lessees, some naturally dependent personalities imagine that this means that it is there to supply a social service of some kind. There is no reason to take on additional responsibilities that lie outside the scope of the company. Reliant people become demanding and sometimes assume rights they do not have. Do not expose the company to accusations of failure over matters in which it has no need to be involved.

2 The appointment of a chairman

The appointment of a chairman is of considerable importance since the role is the focus of all the company's business and requires informed support from all. The chairman is appointed by the board of directors and not by the shareholders. As time goes by, the holder of the post is frequently given considerable influence over a wide area of the company's activities. Different types and sizes of blocks will deal with this appointment in different ways. Usually there is a person, or a small group of people, who have been the focus of the buyout and, with the help of a professional adviser, have to date done most of the work on behalf of the lessees. This person, or someone from this group, is often elected to (or confirmed in) the position of chairman.

The chairman will run the meeting from now on and during this period of innovation and change should coordinate all discussion. Many people attending the meeting will be unused to having to address the chairman every time they wish to take part in discussion. Those that are used to meeting procedure can be impatient with the learning process of others which may to them appear unnecessary time-wasting. In the long term it is not.

The chairman should immediately:

- Announce that normal rules of committee procedure will apply
- Ask that all discussion be conducted through the chair
- Require everybody to accept his rulings
- Appoint a minutes secretary.

If the first meeting is conducted in a businesslike manner, it sets the standards for those who are unused to formal meeting procedures. The importance of good chairmanship is discussed in Chapter 4, where the activities and procedures of meetings are covered in more practical detail.

3   The appointment of the company secretary

Every company, by law, must have a company secretary whose duties are prescribed by company law and which include the following:

- Circulating minutes of board meetings and AGMs
- Calling board meetings and AGMs
- Making annual returns to Companies House
- Notifying Companies House when directors are appointed or retire
- Allocating shares to shareholders and cancelling as necessary
- Maintaining and updating all company books. These will include:
  - the minutes book
  - the register of shareholders and directors
  - copies of returns to Companies House.

The company secretary is quite clearly one of the most important appointments of all. This role is the administrative hub of the enterprise. Frequently one of the flat-owners will be professionally competent to carry out the function, and in many smaller properties this is the preferred course of action (see the recommended reading at the end of this chapter). Larger blocks, or those that have gone in for a sharing arrangement with other similar blocks, as long as they can afford it, prefer to use the services of either a solicitor or a professional person recommended by the managing agent.

A company secretary is not necessarily the minutes secretary. The preparation of minutes has been simplified by the widespread use of the personal computer. Many blocks find that they have in residence a number of people well practised and experienced in minute-taking with IT skills and personal computers.

Other directors

Other directorial posts will develop as each holder learns the role. However, appointments should take into account the benefits individuals can bring to the task.

A good **bookkeeper**, for example, will easily manage the day-to-day accounts, which will involve monitoring the bank account, paying invoices received and keeping the appropriate books.

In contrast, the main job of the director with responsibility for *residents* is communicating. While the increasing use of the personal computer has made this job somewhat easier, it is important that the appointee is a person who communicates well and wants the 'go between' job, rather than a computer freak who will turn out well-produced newsletters in opaque English.

The *staff director* will have considerable responsibility but usually for very few people. Again, rather than pursuing a plethora of fancy personnel techniques such as the introduction of performance standards or annual appraisal, he should start off with what the staff actually do and learn from that. If there is no list of duties, draw one up with the staff concerned, together with a schedule of inspection. Make no promises about pay until there is a working routine with everybody performing as agreed. When you are in a position to do so, pay as well as you can afford, consistent with the pay scales of that job within your area, and meet regularly with staff to discuss a brief set of topics, such as materials, services, security and other problems (see Chapter 12).

An active *building director* should, according to received wisdom, be quite agile, have a head for heights, be inquisitive and of a practical bent. This can quite quickly become a hands-on activity and at times a slightly messy one. Or it can be done at arm's length, learning all the while and reporting from advice received from the company's surveyor (see Chapter 7).

The *common parts director* notoriously has one of the most unenviable tasks. At best he receives complaints about shoddy window cleaning or lack of stairway heating and at worst he has to act as arbiter of taste when new colours are being chosen for carpets and common parts wallpaper. This requires either the unashamed forgetful pleaser or the sergeant major type.

Finally, the *amenities director* carries the responsibility for those matters, sometimes quite trivial, which activate more internecine feuds and quarrelling than any other subject discussed in the normal course of events: namely, car parking and storage lockers. This role requires a practised bureaucrat who has rules, knows them, lets everybody know what they are and sticks closely to their letter. When drawing up a definitive waiting list for, say, car park spaces, and the list handed over by the previous landlord's agent is clearly inadequate, invite those who challenge it to provide proof of their case by producing the appropriate correspondence. As a last resort, draw lots at the next AGM and be done with it. Unless these apparently insignificant matters are sorted out quickly, openly and formally they will remain distractions for future meetings.

Some of the above can be easily combined and are not always a burden.

Directors' duties

There is a range of directors' duties, founded in case law, which all directors of companies should be aware of and abide by. While they imply serious responsibilities, company directors throughout the length and breadth of the country carry them comfortably with the assistance of good professional advice. The following eight-point outline is a useful starting point on the subject of directors' duties for all new directors of lessee-owned companies. Companies House issues a set of free booklets which may be of use to those who have come to this for the first time. They are referred to at the end of this chapter.

> 1 **Directors have a duty not to exceed their own powers given in the company's Memorandum and Articles of Association.**
>
> The Memorandum and Articles of Association (see above) state what the company has been set up to do and how it must go about doing it. They should be seen as the limits of the powers and duties of the company and no matter how good an idea may appear, directors may not act outside these limits.
>
> 2 **Directors must declare their interest when a matter is discussed which may benefit them personally.**
>
> Where a director is either directly or indirectly interested in a contract with the company they must 'declare their interest' to the board at or before the meeting at which the contract is to be discussed. While he can vote on such a contract it is good practice to abstain. Failure to declare an interest is a criminal offence. Also the contract might be voidable and the director could be liable to account for any gain or to indemnify the company for any loss.
>
> 3 **Directors have a duty to act in good faith, honestly and in the company's best interests.**
>
> This is referred to as the director's *fiduciary duty* and forbids the use of company property or information for personal gain or the promotion of personal interest unless formally authorised by the board of directors.

4 **Directors have a duty of skill and care in carrying out their responsibilities.**

New directors in lessee-owned companies will be required to exercise the same level of skill and care with regard to the company's money and affairs that they would with their own property. While certain minimum standards apply, a director need not show a greater skill than can reasonably be expected from a person of their knowledge and experience. Experienced directors are required to perform to professional standards. As the new director's knowledge and experience increase with time, so will the implied standards of skill and care that apply to him. To safeguard the company in this respect, it is recommended that you approach a reliable insurance broker to take out a directors' liability insurance policy to cover the whole board of directors.

5 **Directors have a duty to creditors.**

If a company becomes insolvent or near insolvent, its directors must in law consider those to whom it owes money, its creditors. With effective financial planning, this should not become a problem in a lessee-owned company.

6 **Directors have a duty to have regard to the interests of the company's employees.**

Where caretakers, porters and cleaners are concerned, this is more than simply a welfare matter. It involves having regard to employment legislation as well as appropriate codes of practice. These will cover working conditions, pay, disciplinary procedures and Health and Safety.

7 **Directors have a duty to the company's members collectively.**

(The directors' duty is not to individual members but to the whole company.) They have a duty not to mislead its members, the shareholders. However, if the directors have acted in a manner prejudicial to some of the shareholders, the latter may exercise an important statutory right and apply to the court for redress.

8 **Directors have managerial duties of which some are the statutory duties associated with the role of the company secretary.**

Because the company is not a person and in order to function it has to be administered, directors have a duty to ensure that statutory books and accounting records are kept and that annual accounts are prepared.

> Furthermore, they have a duty to take appropriate steps to protect the company's assets and to set up controls to prevent and detect fraud. So long as the directors are well advised by its company secretary and auditor and act upon that advice, they should comfortably meet these obligations. Properly conducted competitive tendering for all contracts (see Chapter 11) and a strict cheque-signing policy should act as useful controls over the most damaging areas of potential abuse.

House code of conduct for directors

Some lessee-owned companies have felt it necessary or simply useful to create from various sources a 'house code of conduct' in order to reflect some of the idiosyncrasies of the company or building. The lease often gives the right to make additional rules that are reasonable. These supplement the covenants of the lease itself. House codes have sometimes been drawn up following a brief period of confusion or crisis that has been the result of decisions that have been made without taking into account the legal or statutory obligations that apply to directors. This is a good reason to try to get it right from the outset. The following is a model drawn up along these lines.

> 1 All management decisions shall be made in committee, and directors should act together. All decisions shall be taken in the interests of the company as a whole and shall reflect the objectives of the company as laid out in the Memorandum of Association.
>
> 2 A director shall not (a) instruct the managing agent or (b) carry out any work on behalf of the board, unless specifically authorised to do so by the board. The managing agent shall normally take his instructions from the whole board as conveyed by the chairman. The director with special interest in, for example, common parts and services shall be the main adviser to the board on these matters, but his authority shall exist only in so far as he is part of, and has been authorised by, the board of directors, which itself is responsible for company decisions.
>
> 3 Each director will take all reasonable steps to build up a personal knowledge of his allocated area of responsibility, and will keep the board up to date with his activities.
>
> 4 A director shall never use his position to further anything beneficial to himself. Directors shall declare their interest in any matter under discussion which may be of benefit to them personally and, if requested by the board, will neither speak nor vote on the matter.

Company stationery

This is an important part of presenting a professional and businesslike image of the company. Headed stationery should include:

- The address of the registered office.
- A 'reply to' address (often the address of the block, with the flat number missing, for ease of use by directors).
- If appropriate, a telephone number.
- The registration number of the company and country of incorporation.

Some companies refrain from putting the names of directors on company stationery, because of the cost of reprinting with each change of directors.

The address of the registered office and the company's registration number are usually put at the bottom of the paper in smaller typeface. Keep the presentation simple. Use a black typeface on good-quality white paper in 'Times Roman' or similar, with the name of the company in a bold type. Avoid fancy logos: they look amateurish, will become a source of fun to others, and when you still have a full box of them left they will eventually strike you as out of fashion and an expensive fad.

Large oblong compliments slips in the house style are useful. Put the company name and address at the top left and the 'with compliments' message bottom right, leaving as much space as possible for written messages. Compliment slips are invaluable when you want to attach a short covering note to a formal document quickly without calling on typing facilities.

Finally, the use of company stationery should be limited to authorised persons only.

Registered office

Every company by law must have a registered office to which official correspondence may be sent. It can be the address of a solicitor, an accountant, your managing agent or the block itself. It is the official address of the company for all statutory purposes. Yours will have one already which you should ensure is serving your purposes at least cost.

Statutory obligations of Industrial and Provident Societies

This chapter has been mainly about companies. The non-company route to incorporation, that is, setting up an independent legal entity to carry out similar functions, is registration as an Industrial and Provident Society (IPS). The Financial Services Authority (FSA) whose responsibility it is to provide a public register of Industrial and Provident Societies, examines and registers documents in accordance with the Industrial and Provident Societies Act 1965. It is not a regulatory body and thus IPCs have considerable leeway in regulating themselves within their own rules, and the law of the land. The Housing Corporation and the National Federation of Housing Associations, work effectively with one another with models of societies they themselves have developed within the framework of the law. The main benefits of registering as an IPS are that they have incorporated status and as a legal entity can hold property, assets and money in their own name. They have limited liability and can sue and be sued. They do not need to be represented by trustees. Each IPC has its own Rule Book, which represents its constitution, setting out how it must be run.

If you have already chosen this course, even though you are not a housing association, you will know about this and will have satisfied the Financial Services Authority that there are special reasons why you should not have registered as a company. Since you will have also agreed your rules with them, now is a good time to review the responsibilities and obligations registration confers on you.

The Industrial and Provident Societies Act 1965, under which groups of lessees may have become incorporated, requires that there should be no fewer than seven members who will hold shares in the society, usually of a nominal value. These represent the extent of each member's financial liability.

Furthermore, the Rule Book, which will conform to Schedule 1 of the Act, will also have been specifically approved by the FSA and will include the following:

- The name of the society.
- The objects of the society.
- The address of the registered office.
- The terms under which members may be admitted to the society.
- The calling and conduct of meetings, including voting procedures and the making, altering or rescinding of rules.

- The appointment and removal of the committee, managers and officers.
- The number and value of shares a member may hold.
- Whether the society may raise loans, on what security, under what conditions and to what limit.
- How shares may be transferred or withdrawn (if so allowed).
- The annual audit and appointment of auditors.
- The circumstances under which members may withdraw (if so allowed).
- The manner of dealing with claims from representatives of deceased members or trustees of the property of bankrupt members.
- How profits are to be spent.
- The custody, use and safekeeping of the society's seal.
- How funds may be invested.

An incorporated Industrial and Provident Society is a legal entity, rather like a company. It has a continuing existence of its own in law, even though its membership will change as flats are sold and leases change hands over the years. As a member, your limited liability gives you some protection against personal loss if the society becomes insolvent.

You also have duties similar to those of a company, in that you are obliged to submit your annual report and accounts to the FSA who have the power in law to order an inspection of your accounts.

Finally, if a society wishes to convert to company status under company law, there is a prescribed procedure for this too.

ACTION

As a company director or shareholder:

- Check the Certificate of Incorporation and the Land Certificate
- Read the Memorandum and Articles of Association
- Check the shareholders' certificates
- Prepare standard agendas
- Familiarise yourself with the form and function of minutes

- Check that your stationery is in the statutory form
- Decide who is authorised to use company stationery.

As a member of an Industrial and Provident Society:

From your society, obtain a copy of the society's Rule Book, to which you are entitled at nominal cost, and study it carefully. Note matters on which you need clarification. Discuss these with other members. Since it is not the role of the Financial Services Agency to give advice under these circumstances, in the event of there being any problems arising from the Rule Book you may find your sponsoring body helpful (eg National Federation of Housing Associations). If for any reason the society decides it wants to amend the Rule Book, the FSA (tel: 020 7066 1000) would need to approve them and should set you on the right path.

READING

Companies House issues a set of free booklets (tel: 0870 33 33 636). They are worth obtaining for general reading by all directors appointed to the board. The most useful ones, which take about three minutes to read, are:

- GBA1 – Directors and Secretaries Guide
- GBA2 – Annual Return
- GBA3 – Accounts and Accounting Reference Dates
- GBA7 – Resolutions
- GBA9 – Flat Management Companies
- GBA10 – Dormant Companies

Nigel Cox (2004) *Running a Flat Management Company* (4th edn) Jordan, ISBN 0853088608. This is a book on company law in this field, written by a solicitor. It includes a number of useful appendices. However, while it will inform the layman, where your company is concerned, there is no substitute for proven professional expertise.

CHAPTER 4

The responsibilities of management and running meetings

In this chapter we deal with the business of running the decision-making body.

As in any organisation, there must be a clearly identifiable highest authority that makes or approves decisions. Lessee-owned companies may, according to their requirements or preferences, form different kinds of decision-making bodies. The following are usual:

- A board of directors operating under the Companies Act 1985.
- A management committee which meets regularly and reports to it.
- A formally constituted committee of management of an organisation operating under the Industrial and Provident Society Act 1965.
- A sub-committee or working party with specific terms of reference given to it by one of the above.

These should be capable of meeting regularly to manage the property. Meetings need not be excessively time-consuming; a well-chaired meeting can reach informed decisions quickly and efficiently so long as there is a clear agreement among its members that it is there to do business. It is as important to understand what it is to be a good member of a committee as it is to have a good chairman.

Each decision is reached through discussion followed by majority vote. Once carried, it becomes the committee's decision and binds *all* the members of the committee to the proposed decision or course of action. It is the very essence of proper democratic debate that majority decisions are accepted by all committee members. One should not then, as a member of such a committee, act or speak against the decision outside that committee, unless one's resignation from it has been accepted. Furthermore, it is a fundamental principle of ***collective responsibility*** that once a decision has been made, the whole committee will support that decision and work to achieve its aims.

Meetings

Advantages and disadvantages of meetings

It is important to recognise both the advantages and disadvantages of meetings. Good committee members take these into account at all times.

The main *advantages* of meetings are that they:

- Apply joint effort, pool ideas, and reach consensus.
- Reduce, by properly conducted discussion, the dominance of one person.
- Use the specialist knowledge of their members from whom others can learn.
- Share out the workload to members.
- Can make quick decisions (in the case of smaller committees).
- Can involve many in the decision-making and achieve wider consent.

The main *disadvantages* are that they:

- Can be, if badly chaired, time-consuming and at worst ineffective.
- Can become 'power bases' for people seeking influence for its own sake.
- May compromise rather than come to firm and positive decisions.
- Often encourage members to deny personal accountability for group decisions.

The importance of good chairmanship

From the above it is clear that the chairman plays an essential role in the effective running of a committee. A good committee chairman must be:

- Well informed and up to date on all matters that are under discussion.
- Able to inform and explain items to his members.
- Able to run effective, even-handed and orderly meetings that make clearly understood decisions.
- Able to maintain a good working relationship with those he instructs.

Chairmen that cannot conform to these criteria for most of the time are often chairmen in name only. If they survive they are carried by their members, are a drain on the energies of the committee and eventually become a major liability to the whole undertaking. Choose a chairman carefully, one with some or all of the following:

- An experience of meetings
- A practical knowledge of business
- An enthusiasm for the task
- Not least, good manners.

Committee procedure

A description of normal committee procedure should make clear what meetings are and how they are called, operate and make decisions.

1 Meetings are called by the secretary giving notice, either at the previous meeting under the agenda item 'date of next meeting', or by letter giving statutory or adequate notice.

2 Items for the meeting are laid down in an accepted order in an agenda, a copy of which will have been sent to each member of the committee before the meeting. (See example of an agenda for a board meeting under 'Directors' meetings' below.) It will also announce the time and place of the meeting.

3 It is now normal to include with the agenda a copy of the minutes of the previous meeting.

4 At the appointed time and place, the chairman:
 - declares the meeting open
 - calls for 'apologies' from those who cannot attend
 - asks for amendments to the minutes of the previous meeting (except at AGMs – see Appendix 1)
 - asks the meeting to approve the minutes of the previous meeting
 - asks for matters arising from the minutes of the previous meeting
 - takes the remaining items on the agenda in the order they appear.
 - asks for any other business – matters not on the agenda can be brought up by members
 - announces the date and time of the next meeting
 - declares the meeting closed.

The responsibilities of management and running meetings

> Each item is introduced and those wishing to speak are called by the chairman. If the meeting is clearly in agreement, the chairman will announce the decision to be minuted. If there is disagreement, then a vote by show of hands will decide what is to be minuted. In the event of a tie, the chairman has the casting vote.
>
> 5 All discussion at the meeting will take place through the chair. In other words, each member should speak to the chairman and not address another directly.
>
> 6 The chairman's decisions are final and must be accepted by all – otherwise replace the chairman by a vote.
>
> 7 A minutes secretary keeps a written record of all decisions for circulation before the next meeting.

The most frequently experienced problem associated with committee meetings in lessee-owned organisations is the lack of experience many willing participants have of correct procedure. Because committee members are also neighbours, independent conversations are likely to take place. These conversations will no doubt continue to the end of minuted time, but they are still annoying, disruptive, bad manners and unprofessional. A good chairman will always call the meeting to order and remind members to address him, and then only when invited. The importance of good manners cannot be overemphasised.

The second most abused rule of good professional practice among lessee members is that of objectivity in dealing with matters at the meeting. Concern is frequently expressed both formally and informally by chairmen about excessive self-interest in both raising and treating certain issues. According to the Memorandum of Association (or the Rules of the Society), the organisation is there to act in the interests of *all* its members, namely, the company. These problems are addressed and guidelines given below under 'Running management committee meetings'. They have also been referred to in Chapter 3 under 'Directors' duties'.

Types of meeting

Shareholders' meetings (Annual General Meetings)

A shareholders' meeting is usually held once each year; this is normally the Annual General Meeting (AGM) of the company. The following is a typical order of business for an AGM on which a formal agenda is constructed:

1 The notice convening the meeting is read.

2 Minutes of the last AGM are read and approved.

3 The report of the directors is received by the meeting.

4 The audited accounts are received by the meeting.

5 Directors are elected for as many positions as are vacant.

6 Auditors are appointed for the following year.

7 Resolutions for which proper notice has been given are debated.

8 Any other business is discussed (usually if prior notice of the item has been given to the company secretary).

There are some important points to make about these proceedings:

- **Minutes of the previous AGM.** Although traditionally AGM agendas state that the minutes of the previous AGM will be read and approved, they are more likely to be 'taken as read'. Few people remember in detail what happened at a meeting twelve months before and the more general practice is for the chairman to assess their accuracy and sign them shortly after the meeting. They are then circulated to all members. This practice is helped by the increasing use of personal computers and photocopiers.

- **Report of the directors and the audited annual accounts.** These are not placed before the meeting for approval. They are presented to be received. They cannot be rejected by the shareholders because they are the directors' audited record of the previous year.

- **Resolutions to be debated.** The notice calling the AGM will have asked shareholders to notify the company secretary, by a particular date, of resolutions that shareholders want to put before the meeting to be voted upon. These are the only circumstances under which a chairman will normally accept an item for a vote. He may accept at his discretion (that is, if he considers it to be in the interests of the company) a matter for discussion that has not been correctly notified, under 'Any Other Business'. But there will be no vote on the topic.

Some lessee/shareholders wait a long time for the AGM in order to get a decision made on a particular matter. It is therefore all the more frustrating when no decision is made. It is well to prepare for an AGM and make sure that any matter you would like to see the company take a decision on has been correctly notified to the company secretary, usually giving enough time for all shareholders to receive seven clear days' notice that an important vote is going to be taken. The precise information you need may be found under 'Proceedings at General Meetings' in the Articles of Association of your company, which itself will refer to any part of company law that is applicable. In fact some Articles of Association have a copy of the appropriate procedure appended to it.

The AGM can be attended by all shareholders, who may vote on all properly notified items. It is the highest authority of decision-making in the company. If for any reason a meeting of all shareholders is required between AGMs, then an Extraordinary General Meeting (EGM) is called in the same way to consider whatever matters are placed on the agenda. Rules on the calling of EGMs will be included in the Memorandum and Articles of Association.

So that every shareholder is represented at these important meetings, there are formal rules governing the use of proxy votes, also laid out in the Memorandum and Articles of Association. This is a system allowing a shareholder to have his vote cast on his behalf or otherwise have his vote accepted by the chairman in writing.

Directors' meetings

If you have been appointed a director you will be required to attend meetings of the board of directors. A directors' meeting may discuss and decide any matter relating to the management of the company that is not the specific responsibility of the AGM. The directors' powers are specified in the Memorandum and Articles of Association which usually commit directors, in a form of words appropriate to the objectives of the company, to act in the interests of all its members, the shareholders.

Because the company is non-trading, it is likely that some statutory requirements concerning directors do not apply. However, this does not absolve each director from finding out what his statutory obligations are and making sure he abides by them (see Chapter 3).

Lessee directors are unpaid and personal expenses are normally reimbursed under extraordinary circumstances by approval of the board of directors.

A meeting of a board of directors follows formal committee procedure. The company secretary will call meetings either at agreed regular intervals or at the request of the required number of directors. The secretary will also keep a record of items discussed and decisions made and a list of those attending. The meeting will appoint a chairman, who can be removed by a vote.

A typical agenda for a board meeting would be:

1   Apologies for absence
2   Minutes of the last meeting
3   Matters arising
4   Co-option/resignation of directors (if any)
5   Reports by directors (if any)
6   Items for decision (eg expenditure, contracts, lessees)
7   Correspondence and announcements
8   Any Other Business
9   Date of next meeting.

It is the responsibility of directors to make decisions that benefit the company and its shareholders. This sometimes excludes a number of lessees who have chosen not to join the company and perhaps a number of residents who rent. Furthermore, it may include some lessees who contributed to the purchase of the property but who are non-resident.

Under these circumstances many new company directors feel a sense of unfairness about making a decision that benefits their members only. This is because some members might be non-resident while other resident beneficiaries may be actively opposed to the aims of the company or bad service charge payers. A decision that will benefit these may exclude benefits from 'good neighbours' who have not been able to join the company and are in all other respects model residents.

These dilemmas are not uncommon among lessee-owned companies. Nobody can help you in this. You have the information and must make the best decisions you can, always and primarily in the interests of the company. If the company wishes to benefit those who do not belong to it, and so long as the shareholders agree, it is within its rights to do so. But be warned: it is more likely than not that well-intended compassion will compound the existing unfairness and that in benefiting those that are less able to advance their own situation you will encourage others who are more willing and able to take unfair advantage of compassionate company decisions. This dilemma again highlights the benefits of a well-drawn-up Memorandum and Articles of Association.

Whatever benefits the directors may decide to confer, they cannot, on their own authority, give away company money without the expressed permission of the shareholders. These funds consist of income paid directly to the company and, where freehold companies are concerned, include ground rent, rent charged on the caretaker's flat, rents from garages and storage lockers, and what there is in the way of share capital. Neither can they give away service charge income. This money is held in trust (see Chapter 6) and must be used in accordance with the lease.

Defining the authority and activities of committees

The authority and activities of a committee are defined by their *'terms of reference'*. Meetings of that committee must then act in accordance with those terms. The executive committee, be it the board of directors or a management committee reporting to it, has its powers and procedures defined for it by the Memorandum and Articles of Association (or by the Rules of the Society if it is an Industrial and Provident Society). Other working parties or sub-committees, where they are formed, must be given terms of reference by the board or, if authorised, the management committee reporting to the board.

A *working party* is usually set up to do a specific task and has a limited life expectancy. A typical example of terms of reference for a working party would be: 'To investigate, report and make recommendations to this committee by the next meeting upon the need to redecorate the common parts of the building in twelve months' time.' The members of the working party are then nominated, where possible with an emphasis on the personal expertise of appointees. It meets independently, seeks appropriate information, comes to a consensus view, reports its recommendations to its superior body, and usually disbands.

A *sub-committee* is a more permanent body, meets when it has work to do and investigates and reports on a single issue. Again it calls upon the expertise of its members. Its terms of reference are usually described by its title, for example: finance sub-committee, staff sub-committee etc. They are only useful if the management committee cannot deal with the work it is delegating. It should always be a rule to keep the decision-making structure as simple as possible.

The management committee

The purpose of a management committee is to provide a broader based grouping of lessees who will meet on a less formal and more regular basis and, with the authority of the board of directors, decide on matters of day-to-day management for the building. It may from time to time set up working parties or sub-committees to do specific work and report back to it.

The management committee will be responsible to the board of directors but, of course, will not be able to commit the board to decisions or a particular course of action unless it is authorised to do so.

In smaller blocks or houses, the management committee will be the board of directors, except in name. It will be so constituted as to allow others to participate on matters of particular interest. It will meet more frequently and will develop its own practices that best suit the property and its occupants. It will discuss the most important matters and those of immediate interest. When it meets as the board, however, that meeting will be seen as a formal and more authoritative event.

The creation of management committees, on the other hand, is more suited to those larger blocks where managing agents are not appointed.

Management committee membership

The membership of the management committee would include some or all of the board of directors (to provide continuity and leadership), together with a broadly based representation from the whole building. For example, local practice may require it to contain a representative from each staircase or entrance and each representative would be expected to keep in close touch with their constituent lessees. The role of a representative under these circumstances would be mainly to communicate concerns from the lessees so as to keep the committee and lessees informed of one another's views. They would not act as delegates in the sense that they would be empowered to carry a mandate from the staircase to vote on a particular matter in a certain way. Authority for day-to-day decisions resides in the management committee and is conferred on it by the board of directors. If the lessees could overturn this at every meeting there would be little stability or continuity of management.

Committees are renowned for producing silly or conflicting decisions. The way to prevent this is to have a strong and secure, yet open and accountable decision-making body that can make difficult and sometimes unpopular decisions with confidence. Those who see committees as places to manoeuvre people and press incessantly for issues which benefit them in particular and where they can get everyone else to take the responsibility for a pet idea, do not serve the best interests of the company. As soon as the cry goes up, 'How on earth did we agree that?', think it through, identify the individual responsible and come to a more appropriate decision, even if it takes longer to accomplish.

When a block has just been taken over by its lessees, those involved in its running usually prefer to have frequent meetings for the first year, and certainly until the new policies are up and running. These meetings usually take place monthly on the premises, are minuted, and work to a repeating agenda.

Under these circumstances, it is unlikely that the board of directors itself will meet any more frequently than, say, four times a year, with the management committee placing its reports before the board for approval.

Running management committee meetings

Rules governing the activities, authority and procedures of a management committee should be tailor-made and will depend upon the nature of the block and the expertise of those required to attend the meetings. Usually it is set up by the board to monitor, chase, advise and generally provide substance and recommendations for directors' meetings.

In the early weeks and months of the life of a lessee-owned block, during the heady days of the 'freedom effect', some people might seek to fulfil personal ambitions, pursuing their own versions of what is felt best for the building. For these reasons the company will benefit from a ***code of working practice*** that every person participating in company business must adhere to. Usually the code is produced in response to a problem and then companies feel it necessary to circulate it to everybody as a matter of course. Such a code would take a form similar to the following, in this instance for a large lessee-owned company employing a managing agent, which makes its decisions in a management committee reporting to a board of directors.

1 The management committee gets its authority from and reports to the Board of Directors. All decisions made for or on behalf of the company will be made in full compliance with the Memorandum and Articles of Association of the company and the contents of each lessee's lease.

2 The role of the management committee is to discuss, set policy and make decisions. Members will not normally be involved in their execution. They will offer reasonable assistance to all who are employed to carry out the policies and decisions, be they contractors,

> professional advisers or staff – so long as their performance is satisfactory.
>
> 3 A company decision will be deemed to be one that has been passed in accordance with the Memorandum and Articles of Association, is minuted and approved.
>
> 4 Professional advice will be sought when required but only when it has first been agreed in management committee. Unless it has been formally decided to seek a second opinion, the advice of the first will be accepted and acted upon.
>
> 5 Communications from the management committee to the lessees will always be the result of a decision taken by and minuted at a meeting of the committee. It will carry the authority of the whole committee. The principle of joint responsibility is central to all committee communications, written or verbal, and none will be issued under any other circumstances.
>
> 6 Committee members will always declare their personal interest in any matter discussed by the committee. They will not participate in the debate, vote or be involved in any way in the implementation or consequences of the decision.

The purpose of this six-point list is to set out a comprehensive code of conduct that provides openly identifiable standards. It does in fact build upon the code of conduct for directors recommended in the last chapter. It is important to adopt correct behaviour and procedures in running a lessee-owned organisation. This provides for an effective way of doing business and overcomes many problems endemic in organisations where at times (and for apparently very good reasons) hearts are allowed to rule heads in matters of considerable importance. Who you like and who you do not like will always affect judgement. But when, after a long hard day at work, and as an active and committed management committee member, you are helping to decide upon the best interests of the company, the last thing you want is to be defenceless in the face of someone else's self-interest.

Correct behaviour and procedures prevent misunderstandings, demonstrate fairness and act as a corporate *sine qua non* to which everybody present can lend support when one person attempts to abuse a meeting. Courteous behaviour at meetings provides a vehicle for openness and helps the organisation to be effective. Rather than slow things down, it actually facilitates good decisions in the long run.

The absolute importance of courteous behaviour at meetings

Experience has shown that discourteous behaviour at meetings has been one of the most difficult matters to deal with. There will be issues upon which people will feel strongly and opinions will differ on even the simplest matter. Apart from being one's largest single investment, a home is the most intimate 'psychological space' one has and a perceived threat to it can be taken very personally. In defence of a point of view, resident committee members, more often than one would care to remember, have been known to depart from the accepted norms of courteous behaviour and have consequently caused considerable problems for everybody else present. Always support the chairman in re-establishing order in a meeting. If necessary adjourn for ten minutes until people calm down and undertake to conduct business properly. *(You might read out this paragraph, it is impartial and authoritative.)* The directors' legal responsibility is to put the company's interests first, not those of individual flat-owners. Apart from which, discourteous behaviour would not impress a professional adviser.

ACTION

- Check Memorandum and Articles of Association re:
    - directors' meetings
    - AGMs.
- Formulate a code of practice for:
    - directors' meetings
    - meetings with lessees.
- Prepare a standard agenda for directors' meetings.
- Agree the code of practice for meetings at directors' meeting and circulate.

CHAPTER 5

Managerial and professional advice and advisers

A professional is a person who specialises in a particular area of technical expertise, and who has satisfied his profession's ruling body that he has reached the high level of proficiency and experience required. He has pursued an intensive course of study, passed professional exams to standards validated by the profession's ruling body and undergone a term of practical experience in an appropriate professional firm. His status is identified by the letters indicating his qualifications, which he is allowed to put after his name.

He will at all times be bound by the professional code of conduct of his professional body and may be 'struck off' and excluded from practising that profession, or using the appropriate letters after his name, if he is found to have broken his professional code of conduct. He or his firm will carry 'professional indemnity', which is an insurance policy to protect them against expensive mistakes resulting from his advice and to compensate those who may suffer as a result. This is the theory, anyway.

The proper use of professional advice is central to the good management of a large residential block. Almost certainly none of the flat-owners, including directors, will have personal experience of managing large properties. Few will have the time to amass the knowledge required to deal with all eventualities and most will be pursuing their own careers during the day.

Many people, though, will have had experience of seeking and using a professional. Buying a flat usually requires the advice of a surveyor to report on the soundness of the structure and a solicitor to do the conveyancing. Most people who have run organisations, are self-employed or have their own small businesses, engage the services of an accountant for tax purposes.

Most resident-owned companies now use the professional services of a managing agent for part or all of the functions of running their blocks. The Leasehold Reform Act 1993 and the Commonhold and Leasehold Act 2002 have together created an increasing number of legal obligations on landlords mainly in an attempt to protect the leaseholder from the abusive landlord. These conditions, however, apply equally to resident management companies, which is why it is a good idea to delegate the responsibility for them. Fortunately, as the law has developed in this field, so have the professional credentials of the more experienced managing agents.

The managing agent

If appointed, the managing agent will be the professional adviser with whom you will have most frequent contact. Formerly, he may have been a property specialist, managing residential properties within a wider professional remit, for example a surveyor, an estate agent or a letting agent. Today he is more likely to specialise professionally in residential management and may be a member of the Institute of Residential Property Management (IRPM). Many of the large surveying firms have management departments. In recent years the Association of Residential Managing Agents (ARMA), which is one of the sponsors of the IRPM, has itself developed into an authoritative professional body. It has published jointly with LEASE a useful booklet on this subject, *Appointing a Managing Agent: The need, selection and working with them*, and has a website (*www.arma.org.uk*) which contains its Code of Practice.

If the managing agent course is chosen, take care in the choice of individual who is given responsibility for your building. He will have more to do with the property, the residents and directors than any other outside person. His job is to be responsible to the board for the management of the building on a day-to-day basis for a range of responsibilities that may include:

- Collecting service charges
- Paying bills
- Managing the company's bank account
- Communicating with residents
- Settling disputes on behalf of the company
- Handling difficult tenants
- Liaising between the company and professionals
- Other duties as agreed by contract.

Choosing a managing agent

Unless you are a small group of lessees and enjoy a high level of unanimity on most matters relating to your resident-owned company, the best advice is to consider using the services of a managing agent. There may be no need to delegate the whole range of activities to an agent but the complicated legal provisions associated with service charge administration, the restrictive conditions attached to forfeiture and the more active involvement of the Leasehold Valuation Tribunal in this field all point to the reasonableness of using a professional.

You will want to choose your managing agent from a number of applicants. There are no hard and fast rules about how one chooses a managing agent, but it is possible to draw up a list of criteria against which you can assess the standards of potential agents. This need not be complicated or over-detailed. First draw up a brief description of the job you want done and its component parts. For example, you will either want only some or all of the functions managed for you. You may hold either monthly or quarterly meetings at which you will require attendance. You may require frequent communications or an arm's-length approach. List your amenities: boiler, TV aerial, lift, pest control, caretaker, rubbish removal, all current service contracts, insurance policy. List your main problems: the roof, drains, getting simple jobs done. These are the sort of down-to-earth things you will want to ask specific questions about. Outline the main features of your property and the company, listing its directors and their designated responsibilities and saying how you intend to manage the block and what you see as your main problems.

The ARMA and IRPM websites are good places to begin your search. They have lists of members who are bound by professional codes of practice and carry professional indemnity. Talk to local residents' associations. The Federation of Private Residents' Associations will, if you are members, tell you of other residents' associations who operate in your locality. Try to find good local, smaller rather than larger, firms of managing agents with professionals who have good local knowledge.

Once you have drawn up a list of potential candidates, invite them in turn to visit your block and show them around it. Make sure that the person you are inviting is the individual who, if successful, will be allocated to you – you must be satisfied that you can get on well personally as well as professionally. Make it clear to each visiting candidate that their visit is part of a competitive tendering process.

Remember, it is your company, your property and your money, so you are setting the agenda. Firms from all professions like to arrive prepared and willing to tell you what they can offer, and you can easily end up discussing the matter on their terms and what services they can supply while awkward little questions remain unanswered. At this stage, establish and assert those services you want to buy. If they coincide with those on offer then you have something to work on.

Ask each applicant, as part of the selection process, to provide, in their own words, one page containing their appraisal of:

- The building
- The services
- Their priorities for action.

If you have sent to each applicant, and they have seen, your list of criteria before you have your meeting, then the likelihood is you will not spend valuable time discussing glossy prospectuses with photos of large West End blocks on every page. So make your own list of selection criteria and assess each candidate against a list such as the following (you can even use a rating scale for each from A–F):

- Experience of managing residential properties similar to yours.
- Experience of dealing with the specific list of services you require.
- An individual who shows informed interest in your particular property.
- Possession of sound professional indemnity.
- An acceptable fee structure (the cheapest is not always the best).
- Someone who has been personally recommended.
- A firm whose other properties you can visit and check.
- An individual who is formal and professional in manner.
- Someone who can give you a good deal on your block insurance.
- A proven track record and respect in the profession.
- A professional with formal qualifications.
- A practice that can supply other services less expensively because they deal with other companies and can provide economies of scale.

No one will score full marks on all items. A managing agent who cannot answer your questions at this stage and has to rely on his well-trodden routine, will probably not be able to hear your questions when he manages for you. On the other hand, there is good reason to argue that an oversensitive person who seeks to become too popular will not do their job properly.

Managing a managing agent

Unlike a conventional landlord, a resident management company has two equal aims. The first concerns the value of the property, the second, the quality of life of the residents in the block. As one develops a relationship with a newly appointed managing agent it is important to establish clearly that one main aim is to manage the block's day-to-day matters in the most amenable way for all its residents. The conventional landlord understandably sees a property as a commercial undertaking first and foremost and looks to the managing agent to keep residents at arm's length. The resident-owned company, however, will want to get things done to a different set of criteria and will probably surprise the new managing agent with, for example, the tough line it is prepared to take in respect of leaseholders who do not immediately pay their service charge or otherwise abuse the terms of their leases and so offend other neighbours.

However, whatever the aims and objectives of the company are and whichever managing agent it is that has been given the day-to-day authority for them, they remain the responsibility of the company and can only be decided upon and changed by the board of directors. So there are two questions about managing a managing agent that have to be settled: What is the managing agent going to do? How is he going to be required to do it?

Delegating responsibility to the managing agent

First, before considering passing over the responsibilities for the day-to-day running of the property to the managing agent, we should remind ourselves of the accepted principles of managerial delegation. This will clarify the main relationships so that everyone involved will know where they stand in relation to one another.

- **Delegation** requires that authority and responsibility should flow vertically from the highest to the lowest level. It passes from the board of directors to the managing agent and he in turn may now require others who work for the company, to accept his authority as legitimate. (One noticeable point here is that nowhere are shareholders or residents included.)

- **Unity of Command** implies that the managing agent will only be accountable to one superior. This is the board of directors. As is explained elsewhere, the board may delegate a particular function to an individual director (eg finance) who may, in this instance, liaise

> with the managing agent, on their behalf, about matters concerning service charges or annual accounts. But the line of command is controlled by the board.
>
> - **Parity of Authority and Responsibility** requires the person who has been delegated responsibility, to be given equal authority to carry it out. The board must give the managing agent sufficient authority to carry out successfully the responsibilities he has been given by the board. A good professional will know how to exercise that authority.
>
> - **Fixation of Responsibility** states that delegation does not relieve the executive – in this case, the board – of their authority, responsibility and accountability. Delegation creates an additional level of responsibility. When the board delegates, it does not lose its authority and responsibility. The managing agent, however, does receive that same authority and responsibility – and becomes accountable for it to the board.
>
> - **Residual Authority and Responsibility** asserts that there are some responsibilities that cannot be delegated. For example, the managing agent cannot be held responsible for the quality of decision-making on the board or the individual exercising of the directors' duties of skill and care.

There are a number of implied lessons to be learned from these:

- The managing agent must be given the trust of both the board and residents.

- Communications between the board and the managing agent must be effective.

- The board must keep itself well informed and cannot abdicate its own responsibility.

- All leaseholders and residents must be told:
  – what the managing agent's responsibilities are
  – how he can be contacted
  – that the managing agent acts with the board's authority.

Delegation is an art and it is understandable that some directors who are unfamiliar with it will want to be kept informed about everything all the time. If a managing agent is doing his job properly and is trusted to get on with it, he is best left to carry out his duties as he was last instructed.

It can be deeply irritating and time wasting having to answer questions just for the sake of it. The right time is usually the next meeting. All the board really needs to know is when there has been a significant deviation from their instructions, and given the number of possibilities of this happening in even the best run block of flats, the eager-to-know director will have enough feedback to keep him feeling happily involved.

What then is to be delegated? This can be anything from one or two items, for example service charge billing and debt collection, to the full range of day-to-day duties including staffing, maintenance and leaseholder communications. If you are a small block of ten flats or fewer and have a good in-house retired lawyer, accountant or surveyor who is keen to provide a service, there is a saving straight away. Many managing agents have a menu or range of services they can offer in any combination for different fee levels. You can choose what you delegate but from the outset make sure there is clear agreement between the company and managing agent on the following points:

- The standard of works expected.
- A timescale for meetings to review work in.
- Methods by which the managing agent will deal with:
    - questions from tenants
    - correspondence from the board of directors
    - emergency maintenance and repairs
    - any other particular issues pertaining to your block.
- That the managing agent will attend company meetings when asked to do so, including evening meetings.
- That where the managing agent is responsible for the day-to-day running of the block it is done in accordance with the instructions of the board and good professional practice.

When you have built up a working relationship with the right person and he has become an identifiable part of your team, you will not want him to be the butt of insensitive tenants who think he works for them and should therefore accept whatever they demand. These types exist everywhere and in dealing with them, the managing agent and the board should speak as one. All residents in the building will have been clearly informed that the managing agent carries the company's authority and the full support of the board in the legitimate exercise of his duties.

Assessing the work of the managing agent

It is possible to draw up quite detailed quality control standards and set specific targets for the managing agent to achieve, but in all but a handful of blocks, these will probably prove a waste of time and effort. In the early years of the company, circumstances and needs will change quite substantially and unpredictably and carefully plotted targets or monitoring methods will quickly become redundant.

The best overall yardsticks for measuring the performance of your managing agent are:

- The simple feeling that you are getting a satisfactory professional service.
- The promptness and quality of attention you are receiving in response to your queries and ad hoc requests for something to be done.

It is a well-recognised fact that the best managing agent is the one that nobody notices, because there is so rarely cause to complain about the way in which the property is run. But good managing agents are seldom shy people; they enjoy recognition and respond to normal expressions of gratitude like the rest of us.

Deciding whether you need professional advice

Managing agents often have their own favoured panel of competent other professionals (solicitors, accountants, surveyors). If you are taking the leading management role yourself, you will occasionally have need of good professional advice.

Professional advice is usually expensive, so there are a few basic rules about using it. These can be expressed as questions:

- Is the nature of the decision beyond your own competence?
- Do you really need professional advice?
- How much will it cost?
- Can you afford it?
- Are you asking the right questions? The professional's first line of defence when things go wrong is that he was inadequately instructed.
- Do you intend to take the advice? Professional advice is often very conservative and counsels caution. If you are disappointed and disagree with the advice, any alternative action you take is entirely

your own responsibility, and if it goes wrong all the worse because you ignored professional advice.
- Can you, after considering your corporate responsibilities, avoid taking professional advice?

If the answer to the final question is 'no', you have little option but to choose the best advice you can afford and act upon it. You have already taken a considerable amount of advice in buying the property and setting up the company, and it would be useful here to look at other areas of advice available.

Different types of professional adviser

You are most likely to need the services of:

- Accountant
- Solicitor
- Surveyor
- Insurance broker.

The accountant

Two things determine your need for accountancy services. First there is the need for *day-to-day administration of the books*, the activity generally known as *management accounts*. In smaller blocks this function is often carried out by a competent non-professional who is known to the board and simply keeps the books up to date so that they can be shown at meetings and used as a way of monitoring the company's income and expenditure. In larger blocks, where a more formal approach is preferred, the managing agent will provide the service through an accountant employed by the firm to carry out this routine work for all the blocks they manage.

The second need is one that can only be met by a *registered auditor*, and this is the *annual audit*. Company accounts must be audited annually by law. (Smaller companies may be exempt – see Chapter 3.) Since the auditor is appointed by the shareholders, it may be the case that the person chosen to carry out the audit is known to one or more of the members of the company.

The auditor is appointed, paid, and therefore employed, by the company to help the company meet a statutory requirement. The auditor

Managerial and professional advice and advisers

is not an agent of the government, neither is he supposed to be trying to find fault with the company. He is there to advise and help the directors produce a set of annual accounts which are in the best interests of the company, and to examine and sign them as a true and fair record of the company's financial affairs for that year. An auditor must not accept anything that falls short of prescribed legal standards and may, at times, warn you that a particular course of action would be unacceptable. But if an auditor acts like a frustrated VAT inspector and spends his time finding ways to make your life difficult, get rid of him at the next AGM and appoint someone who, on recommendation, will not.

In addition, your accountant will advise you on tax-related issues. Income that the company receives (other than service charges) is generally subject to corporation tax or income tax. Your accountant should be able to give you advice on this.

The solicitor

You will probably already have used the services of a solicitor in purchasing the property and setting up the company. There are only two reasons why you might now need to instruct a solicitor. The first would be for advice concerning **property law, alteration of a lease** or **interpretation of a covenant**, and the second for advice and services in cases of **litigation**.

These are two separate types of legal expertise and it is often best to appoint two specialist solicitors on recommendation even if they are in different parts of town. The type of solicitor you need for litigation is someone you yourself would not like to do battle with. He will have a reputation for being tough and for securing favourable settlements before a case reaches court. Not everyone who acts for you will necessarily be nice!

Again, the basic rules apply. Know exactly what it is you are trying to achieve. Provide a dossier or notes so that you do not miss anything, and do not waste time – solicitors charge by the hour. There is often good reason to resort to a reliable beginners' legal text in order to get a grasp of the terminology and to understand the likely route the case may take.

Seek advice about the property from a solicitor who specialises in property. Give him a copy of your standard lease, together with any other contracts and agreements you are party to, so that he has a full file from which to draw information when advising you.

Finally, check with the Law Society if you have any doubt about the professional credentials of a solicitor.

The surveyor

The two types of surveyor you are likely to need are **building** surveyors and **quantity** surveyors – but mainly the former.

You are likely to use a **building surveyor** when the property is undergoing its periodic repairs and redecorations. For this he will prepare a specification of works, put the contract out for tender to a number of building and decorating contractors and advise the board on which to accept (see Chapter 11). He will usually supervise the works to their conclusion and be responsible for inspecting them to ensure the standard of workmanship is acceptable. He will often be the person responsible for liaising with the residents and, with the appropriate director or managing agent, will often become involved in sorting out the problems.

When the occasion warrants it, a building surveyor will call upon the assistance of a **structural engineer** who has expertise in building structures and can advise on problems relating to faults in the structure of your building. This expertise is most frequently used when a new lessee proposes structural alterations to the interior of a flat or when alterations are being made to the whole building. The structural engineer will carry out an inspection and provide calculations and a report recommending whether or not a scheme should be carried out, or he may provide advice on the best way of solving a structural problem.

The building surveyor may also call on the expertise of a **quantity surveyor** when preparing a specification of works (see Chapter 11). The quantity surveyor's expertise is in valuing the component parts of a contract to give a figure against which competing contractors' prices can be compared in order to check the validity of the quotes.

The letters designating a professional surveyor are MRICS or FRICS: respectively, Member or Fellow of the Royal Institution of Chartered Surveyors (RICS). The RICS will confirm the credentials of any one of their members.

The insurance broker

You will be required under the terms of the lease to insure the building. A good broker will have ready access to a range of reputable insurance companies who can provide a block of flats policy. There will be occasions when you will need to claim on the policy and it is then that the broker proves his worth. His good relationship with the insurer and the amount of business he provides will help to ensure that claims stand a good chance of prompt and favourable settlement. You might opt to insure the block cheaply through a local agent, but he might turn out to be more interested in his commission than in making sure you get full value on your claims.

The point of principle here is, therefore, use one of the large, well-established brokers or a specialist property insurance broker, who can give you good professional advice when the annual premium comes due and who will, if he thinks it will benefit you, test the market for the same cover and a better price. It is often possible at these times for larger blocks to agree a three-year deal where the premium remains static for the duration of the term. Under the terms of the lease, the landlord is covenanted to provide this service for the benefit of all the lessees. Since the broker takes his commission from the insurance company, this is all the more reason why you should make sure you can field awkward questions from lessees by using the best.

Choosing a professional – the benefits

It goes without saying that professionals should be chosen with care. This is particularly true of surveyors, since, if you have no managing agent, you may be seeing quite a bit of your surveyor.

One good way of measuring the interest of a potential adviser is to ask him down to the block. You can then get a feel for the way he responds to the task in hand and be in a better position to judge whether he is keen to become involved.

First-hand knowledge of the block will also contribute to the quality of the services provided. A solicitor, for instance, will do a better job for you if he knows what the garages look like when he issues a licence to transfer use. He may pick up a point of detail that you have missed because you visit them every day and familiarity has deadened the senses. You can 'walk' a good surveyor round your block over the telephone if he is familiar with the building. He will point out things and add to your knowledge of the property if you have a good relationship built up through an identification with, and enthusiasm for, the block. And it is surprising how much a good accountant can save by suggesting that the use to which you put a particular amenity places it in an altogether different and more favourable part of the accounts.

Invite your professional advisers to the building occasionally. Being able to put faces to names enhances relationships. The professional feels better about knowing the client and you will benefit from his first-hand knowledge of the premises.

Professional fees

Like everybody else, professionals work for money. There are competent professionals and not so competent ones, honest ones who work quickly and some who take a very long time. Always ask them how much they will charge for a particular job before you instruct, not forgetting VAT. Each firm is in competition for your custom, so it is perfectly normal to shop around among the shortlist of those that have been recommended.

An *accountant* will usually charge by the hour. Ask what his hourly rate is and how many hours he estimates the job would take. This applies especially to the audit. While it is normal for a new auditor to take longer over the first audit than subsequent ones (because he is having to tailor the job to suit the particular features of the company for the first time), the preparation of a set of accounts for a lessee-owned company is not arduous and it should be possible to get an accurate estimate on each occasion.

Solicitors also charge by the hour, so the same principles apply. A good solicitor will tell you, before he takes instructions, what his fees are without you having to ask. It is becoming more common to ask for a quotation for some types of work.

A *surveyor* will charge by the hour on small jobs, or where you are seeking advice that requires a visit to site. If, however, he has been retained to act for you on a full contract, such as external redecorations, his fees will be a percentage of the total cost of the works being carried out. It is quite normal today, if the contract price is large, to negotiate the surveyor's percentage fee.

You do not pay an *insurance broker* fees; he gets a commission from the insurance company with whom he places your business. If you went direct to an insurance company, you would pay the same as you pay the broker. This, however, does not mean he is hand in glove with the insurance company. If brokers do not get a good deal for their clients, their clients go elsewhere. It is his ability to command the business of many clients that the insurance company recognises in giving him his percentage.

ACTION

- Visit the LEASE website, *www.lease-advice.org*
- Visit the ARMA website, *www.arma.org.uk*
- Draw up a list of recommended professionals in each of the areas in which you will eventually need advice.

- Discuss their strengths and weaknesses with those who have recommended them.
- Take into account location, expertise and fees.
- Choose two in each field of expertise, one as fallback.
- When it is time to instruct, you can do so with the confidence that you have made the appropriate preparations.
- When appointed, circulate all residents with information concerning the authority of the managing agent, how they relate to the board, to individual flat-owners and residents, and how they can be contacted.

READING

Appointing a Managing Agent: The need, selection and working with them – published by LEASE with ARMA. This is a very useful, free booklet and should be read at this stage – knowing that it has been specially prepared by the profession.

CHAPTER 6

The lease and service charges

A *lease* is a legal agreement between two parties in which party A sells rights over a property to party B for a stated, limited period of time. Flats are usually let on leases of ninety-nine or 125 years. It can be sold on to a third party (who may in turn sell on to a fourth and so on) before the limited period expires, but at the end of that period all rights to the property revert to party A.

Relations between landlord (the freeholder, or lessor) and tenant (the leaseholder, lessee or flat-owner) have been regulated by law for many years. In 1967 the principle of *leasehold enfranchisement* was introduced, which granted certain leaseholders the right to compulsorily acquire the freehold of the property. The same rights, however, were not extended to flat-owners until 1993, under the Leasehold Reform, Housing and Urban Development Act. This Act gave many leaseholders living in flats greater opportunity to acquire collectively the freehold of their block and, through their lessee-owned company, to become the landlord.

The latest Act, the Commonhold and Leasehold Reform Act 2002, has simplified the process and includes both the Right to Enfranchise (RTE) and the Right to Manage (RTM; see Chapter 2). It also introduced the practice of commonhold which applies mainly to newly built blocks. These are resident-owned companies where each flat-owner is a member of the commonhold company which owns and manages the property. The new laws do not abolish leases – flat-owners continue to hold a lease from the freeholder – but the law does now provide a number of ways for many more leaseholders to have more control over their leases through membership of the new resident-owned companies.

The start of a lease

Normally, the first lease to each flat is issued by the initial owner of the block – the freeholder. Thus all the leases usually start on the same day and contain the same terms.

When a person buys a lease to a flat they become the lessee and have rights to it for a fixed number of years. If the leases allow it, the leaseholder may in turn lease the property for a shorter period and thus create tiers of leases of varying durations on the same flat. However, at the end of the lease, the property reverts to the freeholder.

Problems with leases

Often leases benefit from being redrafted or completely modernised. Many have suffered from inadequate or ambiguous clauses, especially where the responsibility for repairs is concerned. One of the main reasons why leaseholders form companies to buy their freehold is to improve the lease, thereby giving themselves more security, with the possibility of adapting the leases to benefit those who own flats in the block.

The main incentive for lessees to join the company and play their part in financing the buyout is the prospect of being able to re-lease their flats to themselves for a longer period, in effect giving total security of tenure – for instance, 999 years. But shareholders must also consider what is good for the company. It would be foolish to embark upon a course of action that simply showers benefits on lessees without considering changes that would make the company easier to manage, or without rewording or eliminating elements in the lease that are unclear or undesirable. A well-thought-out package of proposed changes to the lease is preferable. Leaseholders should consider a balanced set of proposals so that when they sign their new, longer lease they will both reap considerable benefit for themselves and promote the best interests of the company. The Federation of Private Residents' Associations has considered this in some detail and produced a useful file on lease variation for its members.

Making variations to the lease

The new conditions will vary according to the specific requirements of the company and the type of property in question. The actual policies outlined under the different headings are of course only an illustration – any changes you may wish to make to the leases in your block must reflect your own needs. However, a typical list of points to consider may include topics as listed below.

- Leaseholders must be shareholders in the company.
- Covenants will be ***mutually enforceable***. This means that the landlord will be required, under the new lease, to oblige lessees to keep the tenants' covenants (see below) – they may not then enforce them at their discretion. This is frequently included when there have been

difficult tenants and the previous landlord has been unwilling to do anything about it. But note the conditions relating to security of cost (see Chapter 10).

- Services will be brought in line with reasonable modern practice. (A building might be served by an ageing boiler which is excessively difficult and expensive to service and the new lease may include a clause requiring flats to install their own independent central heating and hot water, at much lower cost to all concerned.)
- Ground rent will be reduced to peppercorn.
- Service charges may be charged on account (see 'Service charges' below).
- Lessees undertake to pay interest on their unpaid service charges.
- Service charges to be treated as rent (see Chapter 10).
- Landlord's covenant relating to insurance to expressly provide for the lessee to pay the excess on any claim made on the buildings policy.
- New leases will be of 999 years' duration.
- The new lease will be in a modern and intelligible format.
- Any other special rule relating to the idiosyncrasies of the block.

Understanding the lease

'Traditional' and 'modern' leases

At this stage it is worth obtaining a copy of your own lease in order to see what it says. Many still exist in the traditional format which is not always easy for the layman to follow. One might be forgiven for thinking that leases have been written in this manner to provide lucrative deciphering work for subsequent generations of solicitors.

However, in recent years, 'modern' leases have been introduced. Leases can be made quite intelligible so long as you know your way around their general structure. The sense of any part of a lease can be understood by knowing what aspect of the agreement it is addressing and, therefore, what it is trying to say. Be it an old or a modern lease, the purpose and function are the same. However, you may still need a layman's legal glossary to hand.

Old leases appear at first sight to be interminably long and dense, with sections, paragraphs and subsections numbered and lettered in strange patterns down the page. They often put much of the detail in the body of the lease and have shorter schedules at the end. But the structure is very logical and usually follows a tried and tested format which more modern leases have simply sought to organise more clearly. The easiest way, therefore, to understand old and new leases is to examine the structure of a typical modern one.

Understanding the contents of a modern lease

1   Introduction
A lease starts off very logically with a general introductory page, which states the date it was first granted by the lessor. This date will remain the beginning of its term of years regardless of how many people subsequently buy the lease.

2   The parties involved
Next the parties to the lease are stated. You may be the third or fourth owner of the lease on your flat. If so, the names on your lease will be the parties to the original agreement. You will therefore hold the lease by assignment, which means that the ownership has been transferred to you, and having bought it, you will obviously be subject to all its conditions. The *lessor*, the party granting the lease, may be called 'the landlord' and the *lessee*, 'the tenant'. This is normal and will make no difference to the rights and responsibilities of the parties in law.

3   The building
The building in which the flat is situated is then described in its entirety, together with the manner in which all the flats are leased. It will normally be stated that all flats are let on the same terms, but may also say that certain types of flats have particular rights such as car parking spaces or priority use of gardens. The lease will have appended to it a plan of the *demised premises* (the flat) showing the number of rooms and identifying the kitchen and bathroom, all contained within a red line marking clearly the boundaries of the flat you have bought.

4   Sections
At this stage many leases adopt a structure of numbered sections, which helps identify and compartmentalise information. There is a generous use of *schedules* which appear at the end of the document and which are in effect appendices to the lease, spelling out in detail the precise nature of what is being agreed at various stages in the contract. These schedules

are referred to throughout the lease and usually follow a format similar to that below.

- **Section 1**. The *initial purchase price* is stated and, with reference to the appropriate schedule, the flat being sold (the 'demised premises') is described. If you are not the first owner, the price for which you bought the property will be in the document that assigned it to you.

    The *term (duration)* of the lease is stated. Ninety-nine years has been favoured in the past for two main reasons: firstly because, historically, stamp duty charged at the time of purchase doubled at one hundred years, and secondly because the freehold has usually been treated as a saleable commodity for any organisation whose property portfolio plans that far ahead. One hundred and twenty-five years is also a standard length.

    The *ground rent*, a sum you agree to continue to pay to the landlord, is also stated and this is usually designed to increase at intervals over the term.

- **Section 2**. This covers the *tenants' covenants* – the standard undertakings agreed to by the lessee, such as keeping up payments, maintaining good behaviour and giving the landlord access to the flat. This section may refer to a schedule at the end of the lease listing restrictions on the use that the flat can and cannot be put to, and the manner in which it should be occupied.

- **Section 3**. This deals with the *landlord's covenants*, the undertakings he makes to the lessee. Again, the bulk of these may be listed in a schedule at the end of the lease and will include repairing and redecorating at set intervals, keeping the block insured, supplying hot water and central heating and complying with all appropriate statutory requirements applicable to him.

- **Section 4**. A final section may be used to establish a number of *provisos*, which are in effect general conditions under which the rest of the lease will constitute a valid agreement. Here leases may differ and may refer to matters peculiar to the property. For instance, the lessee may be required to hold shares in the management company. It may also state the conditions under which the lease may be terminated by the lessee's default, referred to as the *determination of the lease*. The conditions under which the landlord may serve a notice requiring the lessee to conform to a covenant are usually also spelt out here.

At the end of the lease, as already noted, there are the schedules describing in detail elements of the agreement referred to in the main body of the document. These will probably appear in the following order.

- **First Schedule**: A *full description* of the property being let by the lease; the 'demised premises'.

- **Second Schedule**: A statement of the *rights of the lessee* which are given in order to enable him to live in the flat. These are called *appurtenant rights* and include such things as the use of the common parts and rubbish collection.

- **Third Schedule**: A statement of the rights of *access by the landlord* for legitimate reasons such as the maintenance of services to other flats.

- **Fourth Schedule**: An explanation of what is meant by *service charge*: how it is to be levied, recorded and controlled.

- **Fifth Schedule**: A detailed list of rules concerning *good conduct and acceptable domestic habits* required of all lessees. This forms the *Regulations Governing Use and Occupation* and includes topics such as noise, pets, rubbish disposal and abuse of common parts.

- **Sixth Schedule**: An itemised list of *services that the landlord must offer* and operate at all times. This is a complete list of the items referred to under the section relating to landlord's covenants that are financed by the service charges and thus paid for by the lessees. These are the *Landlord's Obligations* and will detail his responsibilities concerning repairs, boilers, gardens, keeping accounts and employing managing agents.

The older lease format

The older lease will contain much of the above, but will differ because it may have been drawn up many years ago, with all the attendant pomp and dignity of language habitually used until quite recently by the legal profession when drawing up such documents. It may refer, sometimes anachronistically, to different types of services, domestic habits and social expectations. Some specify that redecorations should use types of paint or varnish long since out of fashion and no longer manufactured. Many blocks have now done away with their 'dumb waiters', common heating and hot water systems. Others no longer employ porters to do the same duties as were normal years ago. The law has also changed, and many leases now include appropriate sections relating to collective freehold ownership by leaseholders. Indeed, leasehold enfranchisement will cause many a new lessee company or society, where they can, to review their leases and insert clauses that reflect the realities of modern living.

The main problems for the layman, therefore, will lie in the appearance and technical language of the older lease, which may require a handy legal glossary to help understand some of its contents.

Service charges

A service charge is levied under the terms of a lease by a landlord on a tenant in return for services that the landlord undertakes to provide.

The lease is usually the first place of reference when deciding what can be charged for, how charges may be made and how disputes are settled. But some changes in legislation in this field override leases. The Leasehold Advisory Service (LEASE) publishes a free booklet, *Service Charges, Ground Rent and Forfeiture*, and the most recent edition will explain current legal provisions relating to service charges. These do change from time to time and LEASE is also the advisory body that will provide free information and assistance in understanding the *Service Charge Residential Management Code* which is a publication of the RICS.

Many new provisions in law have been introduced to protect leaseholders from bad private landlords. Resident management companies (who apparently cannot be trusted to act in the common interest) seem to have been caught in this particular net. While there is no obligation on a leaseholder to pay anything that is not provided for in their lease, the complexities of managing the service charges of a larger block are a further reason to appoint a managing agent to carry out these duties in any but the small properties.

The new legal provisions include:

- Additional administrative obligations and time limits on the landlord.
- A range of circumstances under which service charges can be challenged.
- The complexity of settling disputes through application to the Leasehold Valuation Tribunal.

The lease and service charges

- The possibility of prosecution for non-compliance.

However, there are a number of matters about service charges which need to be known in order to understand what is being done on your behalf. Added to which if you are running your own small block with a group of five or six flat-owners who can meet amicably together to decide upon the following year's service charge in the knowledge that there will be no dissent, the following is a useful introduction, while your continuing updated advice will come from LEASE.

What can be charged for

A landlord may not make a charge for an item unless the lease allows it or there is an implied obligation in law for the lessee to pay. And, by the same token, the leaseholder has no obligation to pay for services not included in the lease. The first task, therefore, is to check the **wording of the lease** in order to identify those services or items for which service charges can be levied.

The following is a list of typical service components for which service charges are made in residential properties.

- Cleaning
- Refuse removal
- Gardens
- Electricity
- Maintenance
- Heating and hot water
- Security
- Staff
- Management
- Insurance
- Refurbishment
- Improvements.

While the onus always lies with the landlord (the lessee-owned company) to demonstrate his right to charge for items, it is now believed that lessee-owned companies are more likely to benefit from a wider interpretation of the law and to be able to charge for items not specified in the lease.

84

Calculating the charge

Service charges, by their very nature, fluctuate from year to year. They are usually accounted for annually in arrears, that is, at the end of the year in which the money is spent, when actual expenditure is known. To ensure that the landlord has sufficient money in the bank to pay for expenses as they occur throughout the year, estimates of expenditure for the forthcoming year are made and these form the basis of the service charge levied. Lessees are then charged *on account*, in other words, when they pay the required sum, their personal service charge accounts are credited with the same amount. When actual expenditure is known at year end, the difference between the estimated and actual expenditure is calculated and either charged to lessees as an excess, or deducted as a credit. This, together with the following year's service charge 'on account', is then notified to all lessees and the process is repeated the following year.

Where a lease does not provide for interim payments on account, the landlord has to foot the bill before he can recover his costs at the year end. This has sometimes discouraged a landlord from fulfilling his obligations. Obviously, assuming they are not already provided for, a new resident management company will consider the benefits of introducing interim payments when varying the lease for new shareholders (see Chapter 8).

Allocating the charge

The total cost of supplying all the services is divided or apportioned among the lessees according to the terms of the lease. This can be either an equal sharing of the costs of service or an apportionment according to a predetermined formula which allocates a percentage of the total figure to each flat. A widespread practice is to use an apportionment based upon the old rateable values of each flat, which were supposed to reflect accurately the relative differences in flat sizes. These are expressed as percentages and appear in each lease. Of course, they always have to add up to one hundred per cent; if they do not, the landlord will not receive the full amount required. It also follows that it is not possible to change the apportionment of one flat without affecting others. This would require the individual agreement of all those who would be affected and is one reason why the formula, once set, seldom changes.

A lessee-owned company may also include rules governing service charges in its Articles of Association, but only members of the company will be subject to these. Leaseholders who have chosen not to become shareholders will continue to be governed by the terms of their leases.

Further legal requirements

All demands for service charge must:

- Be in writing
- Be accompanied by a summary of leaseholder's obligations
- Include leaseholder's statutory rights
- Contain the name and address of the landlord.

The Notice of Demand must conform to requirements in law. If a landlord fails to comply with these statutory requirements, the leaseholder can withhold payment and the landlord (in our case, the lessee-owned management company) can do nothing about it until a valid notice is served. Failure to comply renders the landlord liable to prosecution.

In the event that the costs of a major contract are being demanded in the service charge and the service charge demand is not issued within eighteen months of the final payment of the contract, the landlord will not be able to charge leaseholders for the work, unless he has issued a notice during that time warning the leaseholders that they will be required to contribute.

The landlord is required to supply each leaseholder with a regular Statement of Account for each accounting period, setting out:

- The service charges the individual must pay
- The total service charges for the building
- The relevant costs relating to those service charges
- The total amount standing to the credit of the lessee at the beginning and end of the accounting period and the totals for the building.

The Statement of Account must be supplied to the leaseholder not later than six months after the end of the accounting period. If the service charges are payable by the residents of more than four flats then the Summary of Accounts must, if requested, be certified by a qualified accountant. The certificate will say that in the accountant's opinion the Statement of Account deals fairly with the matters with which it is required to deal and is sufficiently supported by accounts, receipts and other documents that have been produced to the accountant.

Because the law states that a service charge cannot be levied on lessees for any expenditure that was incurred more than eighteen months before the demand for payment, as the landlord, you should ensure that you have an annual programme of regular financial deadlines. Such a system simplifies the operation and keeps the board and shareholders focused on a regular annual round of decision-making (see Chapter 12).

Service charge disputes and Leasehold Valuation Tribunals

The law now provides for either party in the event of a dispute to apply to a Leasehold Valuation Tribunal (LVT). In particular, leaseholders who think their service charge is unreasonable may challenge it at the LVT. Complaints to a LVT usually turn on the meaning of what is 'reasonable' – for which there is no statutory definition.

Tribunals (whose members are usually lawyers, valuers and appointed lay people) are asked to say what is reasonable on the evidence put before them and then come to a decision on the case. Leaseholders who have already paid their service charge may apply to the LVT on the grounds of what is considered reasonable. For example, the LVT may decide whether work, which has been paid for, has been carried out to a reasonable standard and whether its costs have been controlled and supervision carried out to reasonable levels of competence. Each party will have presented evidence and will be allowed to question that of the other side.

The LVT can also determine what the wording of a lease means and what provisions it contains for the payment of service charges. LEASE has published two helpful booklets relevant to this section: *Application to the Leasehold Valuation Tribunal – Service Charges, Insurance and Management* and *The Leasehold Valuation Tribunal – a user's guide*.

Consulting the leaseholders

The consultation requirements, namely the requirement in law for the landlord to consult the leaseholders on matters of substantial expenditure, have been changed and extended by the Commonhold and Leasehold Reform Act 2002. Formerly they covered only major contracts for repairs and refurbishment of the building. They now include improvements and long-term agreements such as management contracts that appoint managing agents.

New rules apply on all works where any leaseholder's share is more than £250 including VAT. This is not the average amount but the amount payable by the flat that pays the highest apportionment of annual service charge. The requirements have to be met whether or not the actual funds are coming from the past reserves or current service charge demands. In the case of long-term agreements the sum is £100 including VAT. The procedure is quite complicated and would normally be carried out by the block's managing agent. If there is no managing agent then ask your building surveyor to deal with the notices. It is vital to get them done properly because a failure to do so renders the costs irrecoverable.

> **Summary of consultation procedures**
>
> 1. Serve the Notice of Intention telling the lessees of the proposed works and inviting observations in writing and nominations of possible contractors.
>
> 2. Consider the observations and then seek quotations including estimates from those nominated by the residents.
>
> 3. Assuming the landlord has received at least two estimates, one of which must be unconnected with the landlord, then a further notice must be sent out listing the contractors and quotations received. Again lessees are given thirty days to comment in writing.
>
> 4. The landlord considers the observations, makes decisions and enters into an agreement.
>
> 5. The landlord gives reasons to lessees for having entered into the agreement within twenty-one days of the date of the agreement.

Trust status of service charges

The law requires all service charges to be held in trust separately from all other monies. This is to ensure that service charge contributions are spent by the landlord on those expenses for which they have been levied and do not get confused with other money he has which would be payable to his creditors in the event of his insolvency. The landlord, or whoever is legally authorised to enforce payment, will act as trustee of this separate account in accordance with trust law and any interest earned on the sum must be credited to the fund. The landlord may not treat the money as if it were his own until it has been spent on service charge items for which contributions have been paid.

Service charge policy – managerial implications

All of this may sound very complicated which is why it is advisable to use the services of a professional managing agent to administer the collection of service charges. This will need managing and it is usual to allocate one or two directors to liaise with the managing agent and receive a simple monthly status report on the company's finances. The following action points are suggested.

- Receive a monthly copy of the service charge bank statement.
- Ensure that invoices above a certain sum are authorised by a director. Formerly this often required the signature on the cheque of a director. This is now becoming increasingly cumbersome because of modern anti-money-laundering banking requirements. A director's written authorisation to the managing agent should be sufficient to maintain control of larger sums.
- Keep a monthly check on individual service charge income and erratic and non-payers.
- Monitor expenditure monthly.

There has been a history of leaseholder abuse by bad landlords, which is why many residents' associations have sought to buy their blocks. Most of the disagreements have centred around service charges and these legal provisions are the lawmakers' ways of attempting to prevent bad landlords from abusing their leaseholders. Unfortunately, few of them seemed to have lived in flats and instead of recognising that it is in the interests of all leaseholder directors who manage their blocks to do so transparently and in the best interests of all their members, new punitive legal requirements now apply equally to the abusive landlords whose unacceptable behaviour gave rise to them and resident-owned management companies.

What is not generally understood and should be more frequently emphasised, is that it is not always the awkward leaseholder who causes the greatest headache for the directors of a lessee-owned company. It is the angry tenant who has paid up, abides by the lease and wants to know why one person is allowed in law to delay paying their service charge or to continue to disrupt the residents. As time goes by, one of the most frequently discussed issues, returned to time and again by those who run resident-owned companies, is that of retaining the confidence of the majority of good payers who support the company.

This is why this part of the job will usually need to be delegated. If you are being kept up to date by a professional managing agent who is acting promptly on your instructions, the legal complications of issuing service charges and the pursuing of difficult leaseholders will be properly delegated while the monthly status report will enable you to maintain managerial control.

ACTION

- Obtain your own lease and compare its contents with the modern model above.
- Check the sections of the lease that relate to the supply of services and payment of service charges.
- Understand the statutory rules relating to service charges.
- Familiarise yourself with the company's process of notifying service charges.

READING

Federation of Private Residents' Associations (2004) *Variation of Leases* (information for members of FPRA).

LEASE, *Service Charges, Ground Rent and Forfeiture* – free booklet.

LEASE, *Application to the Leasehold Valuation Tribunal – Service Charges, Insurance and Management* – free booklet.

LEASE, *The Leasehold Valuation Tribunal – a user's guide* – free booklet.

Peter Robinson (2003) *Leasehold Management: A Good Practice Guide*, The Chartered Institute of Housing et al, ISBN 1903208521. This useful book contains a good guide to service charge law and practice.

Trevor M Aldridge (1994) *Law of Flats* (3rd edn) Sweet & Maxwell, ISBN 0752000713.

Royal Institution of Chartered Surveyors (1997) *Service Charge Residential Management Code*, RICS Books, ISBN 0854066438. Look out for a later edition of this Code as it is due to be revised as at summer 2004.

CHAPTER 7

Problems associated with buildings

This chapter is an introduction to some of the problems that are found in large residential buildings. If to date it has not been your business to know, your ignorance of buildings is probably as profound as that of the next person. If you own a flat in a block or house that has until now been the responsibility of somebody else to maintain, there is no reason why you should have an intimate knowledge of buildings. The cartoonist H M Batemen probably never drew 'The man who knew nothing about buildings', but if he did, his satirical genius was in that instance misplaced. Many a good question has gone unasked and unanswered at a residents' meeting because the potential enquirer thought he might look a chump.

Nothing in this chapter is meant to be definitive, but an appreciation of the most obvious building problems is essential if the management team is going to be able to participate and contribute adequately in the decision-making process. Professional advice is, of course, always available and a qualified surveyor's opinion should be sought on any matter that you believe presents a serious problem. If it turns out not to be serious, the fee will be far smaller than if it had been, your mind will be at rest and you will be able to answer questions on the subject at the next residents' meeting.

The condition of the property is a constant and obvious subject for discussion at almost every residents' meeting. Most of those asking questions will want reassurance above all. There will be times when you will guess correctly about matters, but, not being an expert, would rather not back your own judgement when asked for an explanation. Therefore, using a surveyor to establish what you believe to be the case is a valid use of professional advice, which is a good reason to keep a contingency in the service charge for such eventualities.

Many new lessee-owned companies do not commission a full building survey before purchase. The reason usually given is that whatever defects the property has, the problems are already there, will not go away and in the long run will have to be paid for out of lessees' pockets. Moreover, any cash available at the time of purchase will be needed to finance the buyout. Once lessees own and/or manage the block, they will be in a better position to ensure they are getting value for money from professionals and contractors.

Water damage by flooding from an adjacent flat

Water damage by a flood from an adjacent flat is a frequent cause of problems and disputes. There is a common misconception that it is always the responsibility of the landlord to resolve the matter. In fact, it is up to the lessees involved to do so. Again, check the lease and you will find that each resident is usually responsible for the maintenance of the pipes exclusively serving his flat. If this type of incident occurs, the directors should take great care not to compromise the position of the company by incurring costs that cannot be recovered – unless the terms of the lease permit this.

When water damage occurs because of flooding from one flat to another, the lease will usually permit a claim to be made on the block insurance policy.

The policy will often impose an excess requiring that a proportion of the cost of the claim be borne by the claimant. The lease should specify who should meet the insurance excess – the claimant, the flat-owner who caused the problem, or the service charge fund. Unfortunately, most leases are silent on this point. If no help is obtainable from the lease then it is usual for the service charge fund to meet the excess, unless the damage was caused by negligence, in which case the cost should be claimed by the landlord from the flat-owner who is responsible (see 'Making variations to the lease' in Chapter 6).

Dampness

Dampness resulting from water penetration of one sort or another is the most frequent and prevalent cause of damage to the fabric of large residential buildings. Like any other problem that invades the peaceful progress of your life, you want the matter sorted out quickly, and there are indeed a number of things that can be done at once. The cause can be identified and repaired, the extent of damage can be estimated, the insurance company notified, and, in the case of a flood, a dehumidifier can be hired to extract as much of the moisture as possible. But, sadly, in the worst cases dampness in the fabric of the building can cause considerable damage and take some months to dry out sufficiently for redecorations to be undertaken.

Causes of dampness

The causes of dampness in large residential properties are in the main fairly obvious. They can be categorised in many ways, but for managerial

purposes it helps to see them in terms of two distinct categories:
- Avoidable causes resulting from poor maintenance
- Accidents and acts of God.

Through effective, planned maintenance it is possible to prevent the former, but the latter, being instantaneous and unexpected, is acute and urgent at the time and requires immediate action to remedy it. It is, nevertheless, the creeping damage caused by the former that is ultimately the most costly in terms of repair and remedy.

The study of dampness in buildings is a science in itself. Old buildings have been adapted for modern living and many of these alterations have given rise to new types of dampness problems. The introduction of new domestic appliances, materials and modern decorative design (for example, the once fashionable practice of blocking up fireplaces) have combined in the last few decades to produce new kinds of dampness-related hazards – in particular, condensation. This chapter also covers water penetration, leaks, floods and such things to which good practice can be applied to help reduce both the inconvenience and cost of repair and treatment.

Lessees should also be alerted to matters that they are likely to be required, under their lease, to report to the landlord for immediate remedy. This is an important point which recurs in this book, emphasising the responsibility of all lessees and, where applicable, their tenants, to report faults so that they can be attended to without delay. You may already know about some of the problems in your building, but, not having had managerial responsibility for the block until now, you probably have not been able to do anything about them.

To put it simply, dampness rots and destroys. Water penetration creates surface damage to decorations, but its worst effects can cause a serious outbreak of dry rot, wet rot, ice damage to the outside and moulds from condensation on the inside.

First, though, we shall consider the different types of dampness and their causes and suggest some ways of dealing with them.

Types of dampness

Creeping dampness

Water that has penetrated the fabric over a period of time can leave large areas of the building wet for most of the year. The most frequent causes are faulty roofs and blocked external rainwater pipes and, occasionally, rising damp. Chronic problems of this nature are almost always a result of poor maintenance and inadequate inspection schedules. Measurements have shown that damp fabric can take as long as one inch a month to dry out. To put it in terms of the flat-owners' interests, it can take a nine-inch wall as many months before the internal surface in the flat is sufficiently dry for redecorations to take place. All the while, unsightly stains on the outside brickwork and internal plastered walls appear, as salts come to the surface and leave white deposits.

At worst, neglect of this type can cause more damaging consequences through dry and wet rot. Lessees who ignore problems of water penetration in their flat for some months before reporting and complaining about them should be given a sharp reminder of their responsibilities. They are a liability to the building and deserve little sympathy.

Burst pipes

Burst pipes and overflowing tanks mostly occur in the depths of winter, usually following the coldest spell anyone can remember for a long time. Still water in a pipe expands until its mass becomes greater than the pipe that contains it. The pipe splits and, when the thaw sets in, water pours uncontrollably from the split in the pipe. The problem is usually associated with a scarcity of plumbers and the strangely inflated costs of employing one during these particular climatic conditions. When a pipe bursts or a tank overflows in the loft, the water has only one way to go, so the inconvenience and damage can be extensive.

But pipes and tanks are not designed to burst or overflow, so the best approach is prevention before it happens. As a first precaution:

- Find the mains water stopcock outside the building or the first one inside – either will control mains water supply to the building.

- Check the ballcocks (the self-adjusting taps, attached to round floats on an arm, which control the supply of water into the tanks) to make sure they shut the water supply off to the tank when it is full – replace them if they are faulty.

- Make sure all the pipework is lagged to prevent it freezing in cold weather.

- Consider installing additional stopcocks so that separate parts of the building can be isolated in times of emergency.

On inspection it may be discovered that water storage tanks and associated pipework should be replaced in the near future. Plastic tanks are now in common use. New pipes and tanks that are properly lagged should not freeze up. But since all materials and installations wear and deteriorate over time, there is no guarantee that if they have withstood freezing in the past they will necessarily do so in the future. As a 'belt and braces' precaution, it is possible to install a heater under storage water tanks to provide background heat when the temperature falls below freezing. All this should be checked in the very early days of ownership.

Storms and damage by the elements

Water penetration as the result of storm damage is usually unexpected and can be spotted quickly once it has happened. By its nature, this sort of damage occurs during bad weather, causes distress and is a matter for sympathetic and speedy remedy. It is standard practice in many well-run properties to carry out a special inspection following heavy storms. With the cooperation of the block's insurance company, plans can be put in hand immediately for the appropriate works to be carried out.

Roofs suffer the most from storm damage, especially old slate roofs. Apart from being the highest part of the building and therefore the most exposed to storms, many have seen better days. Shifted or fallen slates create holes for rain to pour in. Frequently the smallest damage can cause a considerable leak. When a pitched slate or tiled roof leaks, the eventual signs in the top-floor flat's ceiling can be some distance from the leak itself: more often than not, the hole in the roof is not over the damp patch.

Roof hatches and top-hung roof lights provide an opportunity for instant inspection after storms and many older blocks install them. Roof access is a considerable convenience and money saver.

Ensure that anybody you employ to carry out roof repairs in this manner uses a safety harness in accordance with good practice as set out in BSEN 365 1993 (Personal Protection Equipment Against Falls from a Height). This information is available from the Health and Safety Executive.

Flat roofs have problems all of their own. They puncture, blister and crack. If they are badly drained, they are subject to all the ravages of ice in cold weather, and without a reflective coat they absorb heat in the summer, often producing large blisters which may burst and give the impression of a lunar landscape. Cost-cutting on flat roofs has seldom been a very successful exercise. The worst examples are those that have not been regularly maintained with the original and best materials, but have been meddled with and given some miracle cure with a five-year guarantee.

Regardless of local custom, it is unlikely that the lease gives lessees rights of access to a flat roof. Best practice is to restrict access to an approved list of authorised persons, and then for inspection, cleaning and maintenance purposes only, and to keep the access door locked. If the roof access constitutes a fire escape, install a 'break-glass' key for emergency only.

Mansard roofs can also be troublesome, where almost vertically hung slates or tiles surround top-floor windows. The problem is almost endemic in some buildings where the original mansard window design, though the same on all sides of the building, is inadequate on one of the sides (usually the south or south west). In some cases top-floor lessees may have been putting up with water penetration for years, every time there is a serious storm and the wind is in a particular quarter. A good surveyor will solve the problem, but it may involve a radical solution.

Brickwork-related problems

Pointing is the visible mortar on the outside of brick walls. Properly finished, it is fine and smooth, and slants so as to carry rain down and away from the horizontal and vertical spaces between two courses (rows) of bricks.

When a bricklayer finishes a wall or chimney stack he uses a small trowel to carry out the pointing. This is done to prevent the weather penetrating between the bricks. The exercise is also carried out round the outside of windows and doors, again to make the joints weathertight and prevent water penetration. Good pointing usually lasts for many years, but faulty pointing can cause the outer walls of buildings to retain dampness between each brick course and, therefore, within the wall itself.

More obscured areas are chimney stacks that have been heating up and cooling down throughout many winters, as well as the flaunching (cement base) in which the pots stand on top of the stacks. Standing water expands in cracks as it becomes ice. In freezing weather it will damage stonework and brickwork by forcing smaller cracks to become larger, at worst causing stonework to collapse.

During severe storms, such as that which hit the south of England in October 1987, badly neglected chimney stacks have fallen through the roofs of buildings, causing considerable damage; but these are extreme cases. Again, with the facility of inspection access in the roof, stacks can be checked at intervals. Many surveyors use binoculars from ground level or adjacent windows to get a better view of possible problem areas. Properly maintained, chimney stacks will give very little trouble and fulfil over many years the function for which they were designed.

Rising damp

Rising damp is caused by the tendency of building materials to absorb water rather as blotting paper does. Absorbent materials can lift dampness from the ground despite the opposing force of gravity. This upward absorption is called 'capillary attraction'. It is by its nature a ground-floor problem, which is why most modern buildings have a damp-proof course (DPC) some eighteen inches or so above ground level, but below that of the ground-floor joists.

Some older DPCs take the form of a layer of slate between two brick courses, while more modern ones are made from strips of heavy-duty PVC. Their purpose is to act as a barrier to the capillary attraction within the wall. When a DPC is damaged, or where earth has been built up on the outside wall above the level of the DPC, rising damp can result.

When this happens in a building and dampness spreads in a wall, it is likely that the problem has been there for some time. It is also possible to identify some familiar symptoms. For example, the dampness appears in the lowest part of the wall and there are often signs that where the water has dried out on the internal wall, it has deposited salts of a crumbly texture on the surface. These salts themselves attract airborne moisture, which is why it is often recommended that affected plaster is hacked off and removed. Another symptom is that the dampness itself appears to stop fairly abruptly and horizontally, so that one inch or so above it the wall is dry. This too can be demonstrated by using a protometer (a device used to measure humidity – see below) and plotting the dampness on the wall.

Before spending money on advice and possibly inappropriate expertise, the first action should be to try to identify the cause of the problem. If there is a flower bed or mound of earth covering and therefore 'bridging' the DPC on the outside, or a recently added rendered cement plinth covering it, put there to improve the appearance of the lower part of the external wall, remove them, clear everything from the outside wall and leave it to dry out. If this proves inadequate, you may need to seek the assistance of a well-recommended firm.

The most common method of reinstating a barrier to rising damp currently in use, involves drilling and injecting the wall at regular intervals along its lower length with water-repellent chemicals. Work carried out by good rising damp contractors should always carry a long guarantee.

Condensation

Condensation is caused by moisture in the air inside the building seeking out cold parts of the interior. Where blocks of flats are concerned, these cold parts need not be the rooms where the moisture is produced, such as the kitchen and bathroom, but are sometimes rooms furthest from them, at the far end of a hallway.

Condensation will also show itself on windows, on the insides of external walls at all levels, and close to the ground on the lowest floor. (Here it is sometimes confused with rising damp.) Often the first sign that it exists is the appearance of a dark patch of mould. This suggests that the problem has been developing for some time. But the signs can also be more obvious, such as pools of water on the inside of window ledges or dampness in food or clothes cupboards where the air is cooler. While its causes are very different from other problems of water penetration, condensation can do considerable damage if left unattended.

The simplest form of prevention is ventilation. When water vapour is extracted – that is, the moisture created in the air from normal healthy living people – condensation will not take place. In residential buildings it is a modern problem and is often put down to the ways in which we design our contemporary living areas. Kitchens and bathrooms are obvious sources of moisture. Before the introduction of electric cookers, old open kitchen ranges served to dry out cooking steam to some degree. Before the current fashion for blocking in chimneys, they were left open to the air above and moisture in rooms dissipated naturally up and out of the open flues. Interestingly, the fashion for disguising fireplaces often went hand in hand with the installation of central heating, which has a tendency to dry the air.

Today, double glazing, draught excluders and modern insulation help to maintain warm living spaces where modern families enjoy creature comforts unknown at the time when many large blocks of flats were being built around the end of the nineteenth century. Under these conditions, moisture in buildings usually works its way upwards and out of the roof space, which is both cold and, one hopes, well ventilated.

Immediate action against dampness

Air bricks, ventilators and other methods of vapour and moisture extraction in the walls and windows of buildings serve to reduce the chances of damage from condensation. Their inspection and care should be an essential part of a planned maintenance programme. As a first step in treating condensation, clear all adjacent air bricks and leave the top of a nearby window slightly open. The dark stain on the inside wall can usually be removed by wiping it clean with a mild solution of bleach, taking the normal precautions. If the cause is a damp outside wall, carry out the appropriate repairs immediately.

A very useful device is the ***protometer***, which measures humidity in buildings affected by dampness. It will tell you when a thing is wet and how wet it is, so that you can monitor the drying-out process. It removes much of the guesswork and uncertainty, helping to put minds at rest. Properly used, it can save the time and money involved in getting a professional to give you the same information.

A ***dehumidifier*** is a device used to dry out a room badly affected by dampness, usually after a flood. It is an electrical appliance and usually looks like a cross between a small filing cabinet and a wheelbarrow. It has a removable tray to collect the water, which needs to be emptied at intervals. Dehumidifiers can be hired fairly cheaply and, properly situated and regularly emptied, will speed up the drying-out process considerably.

Consequences of dampness

Dry rot

Dry rot is an invasive fungus whose spores are present in the air and, given accommodating circumstances, will increase rapidly and do considerable damage. It germinates in enclosed, damp, warm areas where there is little or no air movement. This is why wall-to-wall mirrors on battens in bathrooms and once fashionable pine-clad walls in small and badly ventilated kitchens are bad ideas.

Dry rot may start in a cavity such as a box window frame near an outside waste pipe that has been blocked and overflowing down the wall for months. Once the fungus takes hold, it will seek out what moisture it needs to thrive on, and in time its thin tentacles will extend through wood, stone, brick and mortar. It has been known to move in a wall by as much as a yard in one week. Eventually it will manifest as a 'fruiting body' and appear somewhat like a section of a large mushroom clinging to a wall. In some instances, a red stain on the wall can be evidence of a hidden fruiting body. This may be the first sign you have had. At this stage there really is no alternative than to get two or more reputable firms to quote competitively for the contract to immediately eradicate the dry rot.

It seems a little superfluous to say that conditions that give rise to dry rot should be avoided at all costs. The very drastic eradication process involves both considerable expense and domestic upheaval. Plaster and all decorations are removed to a yard beyond the outbreak in all directions, and all affected wood is removed in sealed sacks and burnt. The brickwork is drilled all over and chemical compounds pumped into the wall to kill the fungus, followed by total reinstatement of plaster, skirting boards and doorframes, windows and, finally, decorations.

Since floods by their nature drain in a downwards direction, outbreaks of dry rot are not uncommon underfloor at ground level. This tendency explains the presence of air bricks at the bottom of walls in order to allow a free flow of air beneath the ground-level floorboards. Good caretakers check them and clean them out regularly.

It is as well to seek professional advice to assess the probable cause of an outbreak of dry rot. Where it has resulted from a long-standing lack of proper maintenance, then the fault may lie at the door of the landlord or agent, especially if the source of dampness has been frequently reported. If, however, the source of the outbreak has been caused by internal arrangements put in place by or on the instructions of a lessee, or if a long-standing dampness problem has not been reported by a resident, then, in the interests of all service charge payers, seek advice on the interpretation of that part of the lease referring to the responsibilities of the lessee to report defects.

To put it bluntly, if it is clearly found to be a particular lessee's fault and the lease so instructs, that lessee should pay. When leaseholders or their subtenants cause this sort of problem, it is a characteristic of many lessee-owned blocks to take a dim view of irresponsible neighbours and, where possible, to make them foot the bill.

It should be noted that there is a condition that is virtually harmless and is sometimes mistaken for dry rot. This is 'elf cap' and is a small, greyish, toadstool-looking fungus which grows in damp areas and can be removed. But the cause of the dampness itself should always be eradicated.

Preventing dry rot

The answer, as always, is regular and meticulous maintenance and inspection; being aware of the problems of water penetration and hidden dampness; keeping living spaces well ventilated, all airbricks regularly cleaned out, air extractors functioning, all forms of drainage clear and draining properly; and maintaining a weathertight and well-ventilated roof. Apart from these precautions, each block should have its handyman – someone who is associated with the building, be he the caretaker or a friendly local plumber or, in some cases in smaller properties, a tenant – who cares enough for the building to know where each stopcock is, which pipes drain which flats and which drains go to which manholes and in which direction they drain. But most of all he needs to know what the particular idiosyncrasies of the building are, its potential problem areas, how to get at them, and how to deal with them.

Structural problems

The purpose of this section is to introduce some simple standard ways of looking at the structure of buildings to help recognise when you may need to call for professional advice. There is little preventive care or remedial action you can take yourself if there is already a problem. The first rule is, if you think you have a structural problem, seek the professional advice of a building surveyor. Never try to give an opinion, as it is surprising how wrong you can be. It is, however, useful in the first instance to know what to look for.

A good place to start is cracks in walls. Generally speaking, diagonal cracks are bad, but not always; vertical cracks are mostly not very serious; and horizontal ones are virtually harmless. If you can easily insert the blade of a penknife one inch into a diagonal crack, it will be more than a crack in the plaster and you should get advice.

The seriousness or otherwise of a structural crack depends upon many things; for example:

- Its position in the building
- Whether it is associated with a window lintel or sill
- Whether internal, external or both
- Whether the wall is load-bearing
- The building materials used.

As a rule of thumb, a diagonal crack in a load-bearing wall at ground-floor level needs early attention because it may signify movement in the foundations of the building. This is not always as serious as it sounds. Many structures settle over a period of years, stop moving and remain quite safe. A surveyor will be able to monitor the movement of the building over a period of months. If there is no movement in that time, it is likely that the advice will be to leave well alone, and continue to measure at yearly intervals. If there has been movement, then you are in good hands; the surveyor will be acquainted with the problem and will have had good time to think it through. You have little option but to take his advice.

The causes can be quite unexpected, ranging from the changing level of the water table to a tree that has taken the moisture from around the foundations of the building. If it is the latter, check with your local authority that the offending plant has not got a tree preservation order (TPO) on it or that you are not in a conservation area. The maximum penalty for even cutting a bough off a preserved tree is ludicrously punative, regardless of the fact that it may even be your own tree.

Cracks around window lintels need expert inspection. They might be symptoms of other structural problems or simply indicate need for support. Those in brick which form a shallow arch above the window can be easily supported without removing all the brickwork around them.

The method of construction also has a bearing on whether or not apparent movement is serious. In some buildings, what you see from the outside is cosmetic and, apart from the bricks or cladding directly above it, is not load-bearing in the sense that it is holding the building up. Not all unsightly external cracks bode ill for next year's service charge demands. Some damage is only superficial, needing re-rendering and redecorating. On the other hand, many older mansion blocks were constructed by placing steel beams across internal walls and filling the spaces between the beams with aggregate, a type of concrete. When the floor set, the walls of the next storey were built on it and the next ceiling/floor was constructed in the same way. This is called a 'filler joist' construction. The problem is that different walls on different floors were used to carry the beams, and it is not always possible to know which internal wall was used on which floor and therefore which is load-bearing and which is not. It is idiosyncrasies such as this that makes the advice of a professional so important and why, even though you can make a good guess, you should never take sole responsibility for authorising action of a structural nature.

Timber

There will be a considerable amount of wood in most large residential buildings, especially in roofs that are slated or tiled. The best way to become familiar with what you have is to get into the roof space and inspect it. If it has been accessible to residents, the first thing that will strike you is the amount of rubbish that has accumulated there over the years – so much so that it may be impossible to get to every part of it. When an instruction has been issued to all to remove their belongings for reasons of Health and Safety (again, the lease will not give permission to lessees to use the roof for storage purposes) and you have disposed of all the rest, inspection can start.

You are looking for three things:
- Rot of any kind
- Signs of woodworm
- A sound structure.

A sharp implement applied with force to a good rafter or beam in the roof space will tell you the consistency of healthy timber. It is quite hard. Where wood is of a softer density, mark it with a piece of chalk: you may need to ask your surveyor for an opinion about it.

The effects of woodworm are visible to the naked eye. A collection of holes about one millimetre across and fine wood dust below it, which usually appears in May, are the telltale signs. If it is not a serious outbreak, the wood can still be serviceable and all that is needed is specialist advice and proper woodworm treatment.

Finally, check that where each rafter or beam meets another, the joints are sound and sturdy and have not moved apart at all. Check also for wood that may have warped. If you have reason to believe you have a problem, note it and discuss it with your surveyor. What may look strange to the layman is often, in fact, sound, secure and perfectly normal practice. But there is a well-known saying: 'If it looks wrong, it probably is', so do not take any risks.

Wood that has been continually exposed to dampness and an open airspace can develop wet rot. The wood becomes soft and deteriorates until it is possible to drive a knife blade well into it. Wet rot is not as pervasive as dry rot but will require replacement. It is often found in poorly maintained window frames and wooden sills. Any such signs should be dealt with urgently, especially if they are associated with a load-bearing framework of any kind.

In fact, the likelihood is that, for all your trouble, you will only find slate dust, the odd bird's nest and more rubbish that was not removed. But you will be happier and wiser. It is very satisfying when you find out from your surveyor that the building for which you are responsible was over-engineered when it was originally built and, properly maintained, is unlikely to give any real problems for many years to come.

ACTION

- If you have one, check your surveyor's report to see if it identifies any dampness problems in the building.
- Visually check all the drainpipes on the outside of the building for signs of blockages.
- Ask all residents to notify immediately any problems relating to dampness in their flats.
- Instruct a maintenance contractor immediately to deal with lesser problems.

- Consult a surveyor if you think you have more serious problems.
- Remind all lessees of their responsibilities to report defects.
- Check your surveyor's report to see if it identifies any structural problems.
- Make a tour of inspection with your surveyor to acquaint yourself with the structure of the building and assess any problems there may be.

READING

Jeff Howell (2004) *Guide to Looking After Your Property*, Macmillan, ISBN 1405046589. Widely recommended as an approachable introduction to the subject. Directed at the homeowner but the same principles apply to the larger building.

Alan Oliver (1996) *Dampness in Buildings* (2nd edn) Blackwell Science (UK), ISBN 0632040858. This book is a comprehensive review of the problems of dampness, including condensation and rising damp and ways of assessing dampness.

PART TWO

CHAPTER 8

Assessing resources and setting objectives

This chapter is the first of two that apply management principles to the task in hand. In them we develop a framework within which the management of residential properties, owned and run by lessees, can be understood and carried out. We identify the attributes and benefits that the company can command – its *resources*. These in turn are developed, coordinated and controlled in order to achieve the things the company wants to do – its *objectives*. On the basis of clearly stated objectives, a *company plan* can then be drawn up and put into action.

The importance of this exercise cannot be over-emphasised. There should be nothing here that is entirely new to the reader. It simply puts the ideas in the right order so that groups of leaseholders new to taking management decisions can refer to a simple standard approach to getting things done. It has a great many spin-offs which ensure that the company is run effectively, the property remains well managed, and everybody actively involved knows what is going on.

Resources

Resources are the raw materials with which you work. A lessee-owned company has a number of resources at its command, and it is by using these together that an enterprise starts to manage itself. The main ones available to a lessee-owned company are:

- Service charges
- Reserve fund
- Rents
- Expertise of management committee members
- Managing agent
- Existing staff, caretaker, handyman etc
- Proven reliable contractors/tradesmen

Assessing resources and setting objectives

- Professional contacts, surveyor/structural engineer.

It is useful to look at these in turn to see how they can be directed to get the most out of them.

Service charges

The service charge is the most immediately useful and manageable resource available to the company. It is the payment made by lessees for the services supplied by the company (see Chapter 6) and usually covers major repairs and redecorations. Because of its central importance to the effective management of the block, it is essential that lessees are billed promptly and that payment of the charges is monitored to effect swift recovery.

Many blocks now permit quarterly or monthly payments so that the financial burden of annual payments is avoided. The company knows that it will be receiving constant payments throughout the year and be able to project its expenses on that basis. Careful monthly monitoring is advisable and will pick up non-payers. However, in setting up such a system, ensure that the innovation is understood to be what it is, namely, a concession, and that, in so doing, the company does not unintentionally penalise itself by allowing even longer delays before receiving monies to which it is entitled. A continually defaulting lessee under this scheme should be referred to the terms of the lease. In the worst case, the company would reasonably withdraw the concession and require the service charge to be paid in accordance with the lease.

The reserve fund

The service charge level is set by the company. It is initially estimated as the total amount of money that will meet all expenditure needs in the coming year, and will be held separately in trust from all other monies. If the company so wishes, it can also hold a separate account as a ***reserve fund*** which will be added to each year and used to alleviate the impact of the cost of periodic major contracts. This system is usually popular with service charge payers, as it helps to even out fluctuations in annual charges (see 'The reserve fund' in Chapter 9). If it is effectively operated, it certainly helps to minimise the opposition when the company has to make decisions about major contracts.

A reserve fund can be set up if permitted by the lease. If the lease does not refer to a fund it can only be done voluntarily – but lessees cannot be obliged to contribute. If a voluntary reserve fund is set up, then it is advisable to send separate invoices so as not to confuse money that *must* be paid with money that is being paid voluntarily.

Rents

Ground rents are usually paid to a landlord as part of the contractual arrangement when a flat is leased. Most resident-owned companies reduce this to a peppercorn for lessees who buy new long leases (see Chapter 6). If a ground rent is charged, the money belongs to the company and is kept separately from the service charge in the company's bank account. The company will therefore probably have three bank accounts:

- An interest-earning trust current account for service charges.
- A deposit or investment account for the reserve fund held in trust.
- A current account for the company which will hold income from the sale of shares and ground rents and other rents paid by individuals to the company.

Expertise

In a larger property that employs a managing agent, the board should have adequate access to useful expertise. Your own responsibility, however, will be to know how to ask the right questions and understand the answers. The authority of the company resides in the board of directors. Often a managing agent will do what he thinks is best if he has not been otherwise instructed or thinks that you are not particularly interested in the details. This should never be allowed to happen. There is nothing worse for a managing agent than to find himself reporting to a group of uninterested people who are not informed, and it is a sure way of losing his respect and, worse, best attentions. Always ask questions and satisfy yourself that you know what is going on.

In a block that runs itself, the management committee will probably already contain an experienced manager or two with sound business or administrative backgrounds who are already involved and offering their skills. This will be especially so if, for one reason or another, you have decided not to appoint a managing agent but to handle the day-to-day affairs of the block without external assistance. After all, you have all bought a stake in the property, so why pay for someone else to do something you are perfectly capable of doing yourself, especially in the case of a smaller property? However, a professional who is a lessee (solicitor or surveyor) and whose firm has been chosen to advise the company will not usually serve on the board, as he will probably be taking a fee (perhaps at a generous discount).

This is a learning experience for all. Everybody is learning not only how to run a property to agreed objectives, but, more importantly, how to get on in a businesslike way with neighbours who may have widely differing views. Sometimes expertise can be used as a smokescreen, a way of keeping others at a distance. All the lessee/shareholders have bought into the company and have an equal right to ask and get answers to their questions. The more people know about what they have agreed to, and the better things are explained to them, the more they will consent to decisions and the more readily they will approve of objectives and plans. This itself will promote a healthy sense of shared ownership.

Existing staff

Good staff (porters, caretakers, cleaners) are a positive benefit, a resource. If you are happy with the staff you have inherited, arrange a meeting with them immediately and tell them so. A long-serving caretaker, for example, will know a great deal about the property. The chances are, though, that the most useful things he knows are in his head and any records he has kept are those he has been required to keep by his previous employers, or exist in a little black book he has for his own purposes. Find out:

- How they do their job
- What their daily routine is
- What equipment they have and whether it is adequate
- How they would improve what they do
- How they would improve the building/services
- Where all the tanks, pipes, stopcocks are – be taken on a tour
- What they dislike most about the job (though it may be part of the job)
- What they find most difficult
- Anything else that is peculiar to their job.

Over a period of a month or so, agree job descriptions – written statements of what the jobs are, their daily, weekly and monthly duties and the equipment used to carry out the job effectively. Inspect all equipment and materials and renew if necessary. Let the most senior member know what the budget for materials is and institute a system of signing for them so that expenditure is controlled and not abused.

Show that you are interested and supportive. This is a time of uncertainty and no doubt insecurity for the staff, as they are changing employers and will be somewhat apprehensive about what the new people are going to be like and how the changes are going to affect them. Maintaining the goodwill and cooperation of productive caretaking and cleaning staff at a time when you are aiming to establish a working relationship and raise standards is very important.

Bad staff are an appalling liability. Seldom are they redeemable after a long period of inactivity and familiarity in the job. But they were offered and accepted the post in good faith and have been indulging work habits that have been accepted in the past. They may in the future find themselves doing very well indeed in a new environment and under more attentive supervision, but usually old habits are hard to break. Remove those who cannot be changed. Again, this has to be done very early on and is a matter for you to handle within the bounds of good practice and employment law.

Reliable contractors and tradesmen

The only contractors and tradesmen that come into this category are those who:

- Have worked regularly on the building
- Have carried out work to acceptable standards
- Have returned and rectified faulty work without charge
- Have readily worked to a fixed price
- Have usually completed on time
- Have been neither expensive nor inexpensive.

The qualifications are about the same as those for continuing to employ anybody in a normal responsible job. If you are responsible for 'maintenance' through your role, and you know of such a firm, it is to be cherished and its top man treated in the same way as you would treat a good employee.

Let the appointed supervisor supervise the work. It is unwise to become involved with the supervision of contractors and tradesmen on site. Because the normal employer/employee relationship in the building trade is an autocratic one, they should be judged on performance alone. So long as your 'Standard Conditions for Contractors' (see Appendix 2B) are part of the contract you have with them, your interests should be

Assessing resources and setting objectives

well taken care of. But make sure you are available to be contacted in case your advice or authorisation is required. Progress can grind to a halt if authorisation for a solution to a problem is needed and is not available.

Establishing a good relationship with contractors and tradesmen is, of course, a two-way process. The surest contribution that you can make – thereby ensuring their best attentions – is *to pay on time, every time*. Two conditions apply here. First, never instruct a contractor without knowing you have adequate money in the bank to pay him. Secondly, put your accountant/financial director on notice that you will require payments to be made swiftly.

However, it is up to you to make it abundantly clear to the contractor or tradesman that the work must be properly inspected before the invoice is passed for payment. This will be respected and, allowing for the inevitable odd misunderstanding, you will have one of the most valuable resources available.

Professionals

A good professional (surveyor, accountant, solicitor) can be measured by:

- How much personal interest he shows in the company, its members and the property.
- How promptly and effectively he deals with your queries.
- How worried you would be if you knew he was on the other side in a dispute requiring professional representation.

As has been suggested, smaller local firms are to be preferred, as you are more likely to get the attentions of a senior person who knows the area and its local by-laws and will bring more personal experience and expertise to the relationship.

Additional important information

A great deal more information is available to you than is first apparent. It is normal when taking over from a previous landlord, or indeed when a managing agent takes over from an outgoing one, to require your predecessor to pass on to you plans, lists and other documents relating to the property (RTM companies are entitled to this before the acquisition date – see Chapter 2). These will assist a smoother handover and act as useful resources. Much of this information will be of practical use, not only in settling subsequent inter-flat disputes going back to a time before you were in charge, but also in clarifying particular idiosyncrasies of the building – such as why some drains get blocked all the time while others do not. They form a useful resource that can help save time and money in solving problems.

The main sources of further information are:

From the former managing agent:

- All previous accounts and books.
    - details of expenditure for current financial year
    - current budget figures
    - copies of past three years' financial reports
    - name and contact information of present auditor.
- Employees
    - contracts of employment
    - tax records
    - P45
    - disciplinary records.
- Maintenance
    - manual
    - lifts
    - boiler
    - fuel supply
    - building
    - window cleaning
    - entry phone
    - TV aerial/satellite dish/cable.
- Security
    - door entry system
    - alarms
    - keys.
- Insurance
    - employer's liability
    - occupier's liability

Assessing resources and setting objectives

- buildings
- contents
- boilers
- lifts.
- Professional information
  - initial architect's drawings of the property
  - previous reports on the property, eg surveyor's
  - name of accountant or solicitor.
- Drawings of approved alterations to flats
  - copies of licences granted to tenants for alterations.
- Leaseholders
  - names, addresses and phone numbers of all lessees
  - lists of amenities used by lessees, eg parking
  - rents charged for amenities, eg storage
  - lessees' waiting lists for amenity renting/use.

From the local authority:

- Drain plan if available (more useful than you might suppose)
- District surveyor's approvals of structural alterations, if available
- Recent planning applications and approvals
- Environmental notices received.

There may be further information available specific to your property. If it is available, this is the right time to obtain it. It is with this information that you can move forward to look at the ***objectives*** of the company.

Aims and objectives

The overall ***business aim*** of a company can be expressed in a single sentence which describes its purpose as laid down in its Memorandum of Association. That of a lessee-owned company might read:

> *'The aim of this company is to manage XYZ Mansions in the specific interests of its shareholders by maintaining to a good standard the fabric and appearance of the building and therefore its value and the quality of life of its residents.'*

Its *business objectives* are separate statements about how it intends setting targets or goals to achieve the aim. Business objectives have many functions and some of these can be listed as follows:

- To give *direction* to the activities of the company
- To provide an *agenda* of matters to be dealt with
- To *coordinate* the efforts of those involved
- To create a coherent *policy* for action
- To ensure that information is properly *communicated* to members.

Objectives therefore serve two important functions in a lessee-owned company. First, they state what has been collectively agreed and is collectively intended. Secondly, they provide a method for agreeing things. They are therefore an important focus when you are trying to get a number of people to arrive at and agree a company decision.

The areas in which objectives are normally set can be listed as follows.

- Development of the property
- Managerial performance (of the managing agent or management committee)
- Income and expenditure
- Planned maintenance
- Staff
- Amenities and services.

The company is in existence to create and sustain value. It is not in business to make a profit, although it may show a surplus at year end. Profit-oriented business objectives do not apply. From the start, all objectives should focus on raising or maintaining standards in order to ensure, on the one hand, that the value of the property is maintained and, on the other, that leaseholders are getting value for money from their service charge. Lessee-owned companies often seek to improve and sustain quality and this is reflected in their business objectives.

The following are areas where objectives have to be set and therefore information has to be collected.

Assessing resources and setting objectives

Development of the property

Refurbishments and redecorations are not only part of the landlord's covenants: they are what give the property its public image. Good standards here can add value to the flats themselves. They also demonstrate to service charge payers that the company has been successful in improving the property. To achieve this, the appropriate resources are:

- A good surveyor
- All available drawings and plans of the block
- Information on previous alterations from the maintenance manual
- The previous specification for the same works
- The drain plan.

Managerial performance (managing agent)

The management committee or managing agent will have responsibility for the day-to-day running of the property. Both a managing agent and the management committee will want to know whether what they have achieved is satisfactory. Standards of achievement in terms of timescales and budgets can be put on most managerial jobs.

Income and expenditure

This category lends itself the best of all to setting objectives and measuring results. Annual estimates provide a forecast of expenditure in clear categories. At the end of the year, actual income and expenditure can be compared with that year's forecast figures. To monitor this, a simple form of budgetary control can be introduced and referred to throughout the year to monitor major items of expenditure against the previous year. Useful information here would be:

- Previous accounts
- Management letters from auditors
- Where possible, files on major projects, service charges, wages and other employment costs, fees, electricity, water, gas, professional, etc.

Planned maintenance

This refers to the annual cycle of periodic inspection and repair. Good planned maintenance should be based upon an inspection and maintenance manual drawn up specifically for the building. This should include an inventory of:

- All items to be inspected, maintained or renewed
- The frequency of inspection, maintenance and renewal of each
- Method of inspection and maintenance
- Maintenance companies with whom you have contracts.

The manual will contain the appropriate quality standards, and the outcome of each periodic inspection should be reported to the board of directors. If not already established, the information you need to set up this procedure would come from the surveyor's report on the building, copies of records of previous work carried out, and any previous records of planned maintenance. Since this only needs to be written once, this is another item where the help of a local surveyor would be useful. The management objective of the exercise is to establish a way of knowing that all maintenance has been carried out at the right time and to the right standards.

Staff

Staff objectives can best be laid down in lists of duties. The duties of cleaners can be simply described, while those of the caretaker would need a more comprehensive job description. Duty lists would refer specifically to:

- What each member of staff does
- How often they do it
- To what standards.

Lists of duties should be drawn up with the staff concerned who should also be involved in setting acceptable standards. Staff have more incentive to work to rules they have had a hand in making than those which are imposed. This is important in order to avoid resentment. The purpose of setting staff objectives is to ensure that someone is responsible for every task that needs to be done and that they know what standard is acceptable. If available, copies of staff records, attendance records, past and current rates of pay and job descriptions can all help here. The usual method of monitoring staff performance is by inspection and regular meetings with staff.

Assessing resources and setting objectives

Amenities and services

The company may administer a number of amenities such as garages and storage spaces that it lets out separately to individual leaseholders for which separate rents are charged. These are usually not included in the individual leases. Even though they can be the cause of considerable disagreement and conflict, they should be very easy to administer once the initial objectives have been agreed. This will depend on present users, the waiting list and the terms of the contract.

The main objective here is to establish: a definitive waiting list for each type of amenity (eg garage or store); current usage of each amenity; current rents; entitlement of each user; and bring practice in line with existing contracts.

If you could obtain from the previous managers a written declaration confirming the accuracy of the information they pass over to you, it would help avoid having to reconcile time-consuming disagreements at a later date. Check the form of contract. If it is periodically renewable, and there are notable anomalies of practice, your company may decide to change aspects of the letting policy concerning safety, inspection, use and circumstances under which contracts would be terminated. Obviously, the new terms could only be introduced as each contract expired. Where rents have been nominal, you may consider introducing market rents for amenities. This would give a proper return for the company and create a realistic waiting list.

The company will inherit the landlord's liability for repairs of all amenities that will have to be kept in good order. These will usually be paid out of income from amenities. These responsibilities are generally found in the main lease, since the landlord is the freeholder, and probably repeated in the separate amenity contracts.

The main objective will be to keep the amenities in good order so that they continue to bring in added income and at least pay for themselves. This will normally depend upon periodic inspection. Again, unless it is perfectly obvious what has to be done, a surveyor's report will establish the current state of their maintenance.

Setting objectives

Eventually you will be able to set down a simple list of objectives that the company intends to achieve. This may be the time to create a 'wish list' of all the contributions and ideas from residents. Some may be immediately achievable, but the others will need to be included in the list of objectives. 'Good ideas' do not always make useful objectives. It may already be obvious to you what you want to achieve and what type of business objectives you want to set. However, before establishing them, a useful mental discipline is to apply the following five criteria to any objective or group of objectives you decide to adopt.

---

1. An objective should be **measurable**. The standard used can be money, time, cost, quantity or quality. Unless an objective is capable of being measured, there is no way of knowing whether it has been achieved and therefore whether it was cost-effective.

2. An objective should be **attainable**. Unless there is a realistic chance of attaining the objective, it will not be an incentive and time, effort and money (resources) will be wasted. On the other hand, setting moderate standards is a waste of valuable resources. The right balance is somewhere between an achievable level of difficulty and assured value for money. Objectives that cannot be attempted now may be much easier when the financial situation is healthier in years to come.

3. An objective should be **acceptable**. Acceptability implies consent and support by those participating. Participation is a useful tool here. When lessees are involved, they expect their participation to be effective and it often is. When the majority opinion supports a course of action, failure brings recrimination only from the minority. A bad reason to promote the principle of attainability, perhaps, but a newly formed group of lessees with high hopes can be volatile.

4. An objective should be **compatible** with other objectives you have set. They should support one another and not conflict. The main sources of conflict in a residential building stem from the opposing views and interests of residents. One way of dealing with these is to insist that objectives be compatible and that the interests of the company are paramount.

5. An objective should take into account **opportunity cost**. There is often an element of 'trade-off' when setting objectives and this simply reflects an imperfect world. Simply stated, if we spend our limited financial resources on mending the roof, the unsightly garden will have to wait.

It is important here to emphasise the point that a 'good idea' does not necessarily make a sound business objective. In those 'Let's do so and so' discussions when some very 'good ideas' are beginning to be enthusiastically discussed and taken seriously by a surprising number of people, invite them to apply the five criteria above so that they might be

Assessing resources and setting objectives

put forward for agreement as business objectives.

A disgruntled resident will ask, sometimes many months after a decision has been fully discussed and taken, why such and such was given priority or indeed continues to be given priority. A clearly stated list of objectives openly agreed from the outset, written down and circulated, focusing on the needs of the company and based on sound managerial principles, helps avoid serious misunderstandings. Writing down objectives avoids problems later. What you can remember now is often not precisely what happened or was decided at the time. These five criteria provide a check for the likely effectiveness of your objectives. Make a clear record of your decisions and stick to them until they are reviewed and revised in the proper way.

Getting consent for objectives

Decisions are very seldom unanimous. If you are locked in initial disagreement you need to get all the cards on the table so that everybody can play a part in comparing their problem areas on equal terms. Quickly taken votes, however expedient at the time, often lead to further problems and people can feel railroaded, especially if they believe their views have not been given a proper hearing or something has not been properly explained. Yet unless there is a consensus, even though it may only have to be a simple majority, discussion can get bogged down and lose impetus. Lessees' meetings may not require highly sophisticated methods of decision-making, but they do need to be run with care if effective and lasting consent is to be achieved.

Most managers have their own tried and tested ways of gathering information, presenting it and getting a decision, but two useful ones are offered here which would be used to good effect in very different circumstances.

1 Transferable vote

The first, especially useful where matters of taste are being debated, is to offer three alternative plans, colour charts or choices and apply a simple form of voting which allows the participants to identify their two most favoured choices in order of preference out of the three on offer. While this does not always work, especially if the first choices split evenly, it is usually found that most of the second choice votes are cast for the least objectionable option and a majority is achieved. At worst this reflects an overall disinclination for one alternative, and at best a clear preference for another.

2 The LIP model

By contrast, agreeing on priorities where the expenditure of thousands of pounds is involved calls for an altogether more analytical approach where everybody concerned can take some time to talk through alternatives in a structured way. The ***Location–Intensity–Priority*** (LIP) device (see **Figure 2**) is a useful method which can identify or locate each of the available and competing alternative problems demanding attention and set them down on one sheet of paper. It then provides a means of assessing their comparative importance or relative intensity as problems. This in turn should produce a pattern or display that helps the meeting decide its priorities and agree upon a course of action.

The device does not provide a cut-and-dried answer to a problem. Rather it is a tool to assist the decision-makers. The LIP model helps groups of individuals to discuss problems from data they themselves generate and therefore can agree with. It may be useful to use a flip chart or white board so that all present can see the same image.

The method has three stages:

The **first stage** is a simple matrix or grid which can be as limited or extensive as required. One of the main attractions of this is that it is easily adapted to different circumstances. On the vertical axis, problem areas can be displayed (roof, lifts, cleaning). On the horizontal axis, possible remedies can be suggested (repair, maintain, report, contract, cancel). The matrix should be built up with information that is specifically appropriate to the needs of the building and the landlord's responsibilities. The squares on the matrix can now be used to identify or 'locate' known problem areas and their appropriate remedies.

The **second stage** is the most contentious and focuses discussion on how serious a problem is. This is the heart of the whole process and allows for only four alternatives. These are:

1 A problem with less serious consequences with a more available solution.

2 A problem with less serious consequences with a less available solution.

3 A problem with more serious consequences with a more available solution.

4 A problem with more serious consequences with a less available solution.

Assessing resources and setting objectives

FIGURE 2 **Location–Intensity–Priority**

ITEMS \ ACTION	Repair	Remove	Replace	Instruct surveyor to report	Buy	Contract		
Roof								
Pipework								
Lifts								
Common parts								
Staff								
Car parking								

More serious consequences

More available solution — **3** | **4** — Less available solution

1 | **2**

Less serious consequences

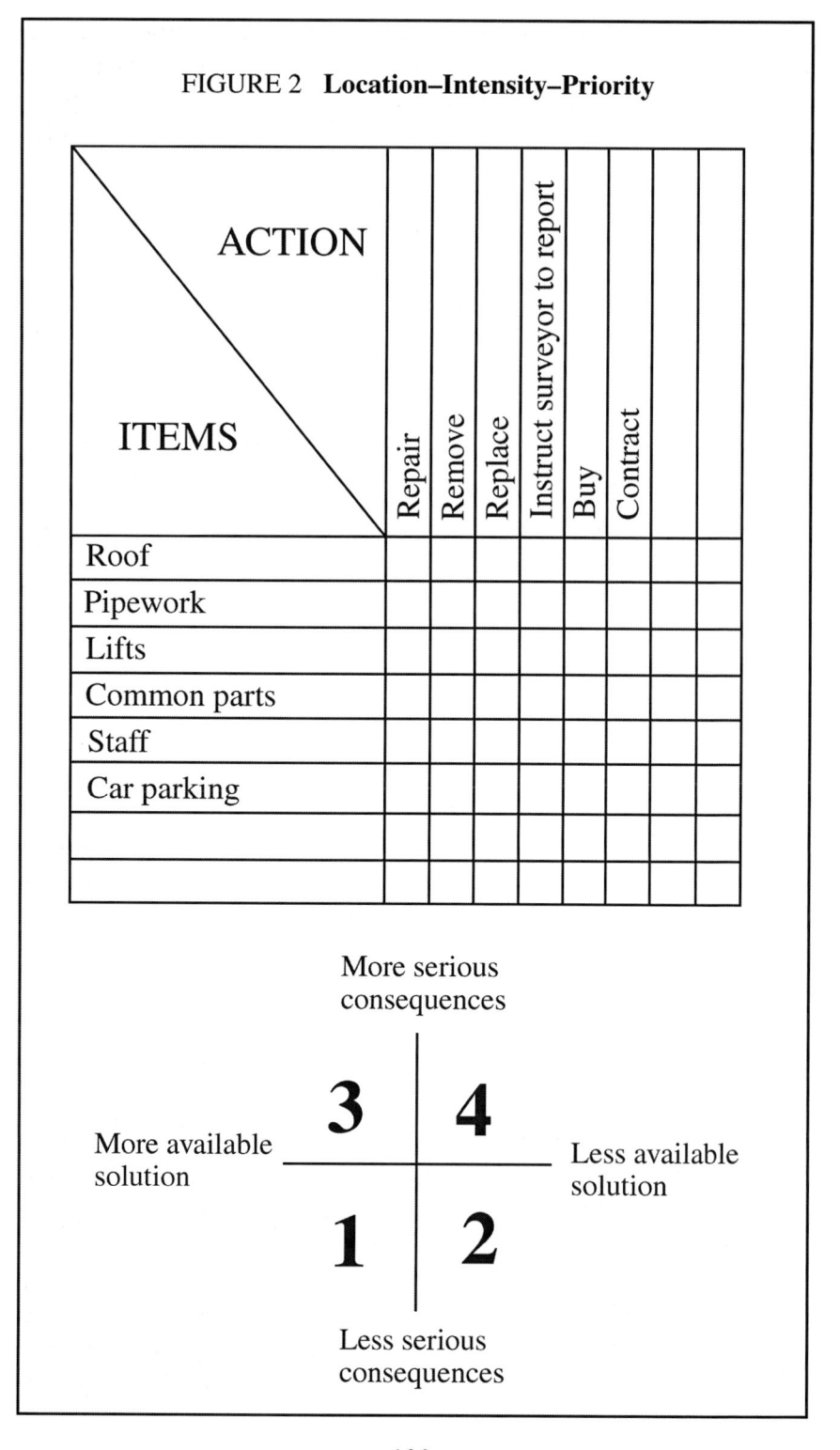

120

Clearly these are in increasing order of intensity as problems. They might be weighted 1, 2, 3 and 4. Each of the squares on the grid that can be identified as being problem areas, are now allocated the appropriate weighting or 'intensity' (1, 2, 3 or 4) – after a discussion of each has produced a majority agreement. As a result, the most serious problems are usually emphasised and can be seen in relation to all the others so that they can be allocated a 'priority'.

Openly discussed and clearly set out, this process can help a meeting come to a consensus on what its real priorities are. The outcome is very often a considerable surprise. For example, not only are the most serious problems identified and agreed upon, but hitherto unexpected connections between them can be revealed that explain the existence of age-old problems caused by the innocent abuse of services. An example might be a flat that has inappropriately taken its additional central heating off the communal hot water supply instead of the heating system and therefore enjoys 'hot heating' in summer and 'cold heating' in winter. If the meeting has been well informed and handled sensitively, all present have had a chance to contribute to the outcome and will consent to the eventual list of objectives.

The **third stage** is simply to draw up a record of your collective decisions, which will form the basis of your objectives. Support them with a clear statement of the reasons why they have been made. It is also useful to supplement this with a statement of the consequences of *not* taking these decisions.

Those who cannot be convinced (and there are often one or two) must at least be clear that the majority has considered and rejected alternative courses of action *because of their likely consequences.* Conversely, what initially may be an uncomfortable course of action for everybody has been accepted because the consequences of doing either nothing or something else have been found to be unacceptable by the majority. For example, failure to mend the roof immediately will lead to greater expense when it deteriorates further or causes dry rot.

But it might not stop there. Beware the insistent, 'deep and confident voice' of the individual who, absent at the last meeting when a good and seriously considered decision had been taken, wants to change it by force of personality. Avoid the 'compromise decision syndrome', where a good decision is changed and no one person (eg the deep and confident voice) sees themselves as individually responsible for the new and daft decision because, although confused, everybody agreed. Some of the most ludicrous decisions have been made by ill-informed people sitting around tables, in discussions that are half understood and who feel they have

Assessing resources and setting objectives

justified the time they have spent sitting opposite each other simply by agreeing to something. Good decisions are sometimes difficult to arrive at and require firm chairmanship, good information, participation and teamwork.

List the decisions you have made clearly in order of priority. Make sure that they are agreed and minuted at the next directors' meeting so they become company policy. This will feed into the activities content of the *rolling plan* (see Chapter 9). Together they will form the basis of the strategy, which in turn will be an indication not only of *what* you intend to do, but *how*, *when* and *with what* you intend to do it.

Constraints on objectives

There are three influences that determine what the company as landlord must and must not do. They are the law, the Memorandum and Articles of Association of the company, and the lease (and in particular the landlord's covenants).

As far as *company law* is concerned, you will have met most of its requirements by setting up the company properly and especially by appointing a good company secretary. However, as the landlord you are responsible for Health and Safety, employment law, fire regulations, and other statutory requirements if you employ a caretaker and/or cleaners (see Chapter 12). The value of a good managing agent cannot be emphasised enough here, since he will be expected to act for the company in all these matters and advise as appropriate.

The *Memorandum and Articles of Association* will limit you to the declared purposes for which the company was set up. Unless of course it is specifically stated, you will not, for instance, be a property developer with the objectives of buying out the rest of the road. The Memorandum and Articles of Association will not feature prominently in the setting of management objectives except in so far as they indicate the overall business aims of the company.

The *lease* requires the company to observe the landlord's covenants. There may be outstanding problems that you considered it not worth pressing your former landlord over while there was a chance of buying the freehold. You may have taken over while a contract was in progress and which must now be seen through to completion. The landlord's covenants in the lease will state how often major redecorations must be carried out, and one group of lessees may have been pressing all along for these to be carried out, knowing that the company will find it hard to resist once the freehold has been bought.

ACTION

Using the information in this chapter:

- Make a list of all the resources available to the company
- Decide how they may be developed or improved
- Allocate priorities to them (eg via the LIP model)
- Agree objectives in the main areas described
- Have all agreed business objectives submitted to and minuted at board level.

CHAPTER 9

Planning strategy

This chapter is of particular use to smaller resident companies or those who for one reason or another have chosen not to appoint a managing agent and have decided to adapt their own expertise to the task of property management. The principles may not be new to everybody but it is a useful discussion and exercise to follow through. Some extraordinarily prudent groups of lessees will wish to carry out this exercise before embarking upon the purchase of the property. But a full planning exercise should be, and usually is, carried out when the company is formed and the property is lessee-owned.

Why devise a plan?

The purpose of a plan is to give ordered momentum, direction and control to your objectives and to create conditions in which they can be achieved. In a lessee-owned company a plan is also a way of demonstrating to members that a systematic and businesslike approach is being taken to the management of what is probably their most valuable asset.

As any experienced manager will confirm, the three basic questions most planners ask are:

- Where are we?
- Where do we want to be?
- How do we get there?

More specifically, when the lessee/shareholders want to know that the way ahead has been mapped out, especially when there is a need to confirm a sense of security among members in the early days, a plan answers perennial questions such as:

- In what order are things going to be done?
- What is the money going to be spent on?
- Who is going to advise?
- When will the work be done?

- Who will be doing the work?
- Is it going to disrupt our lives?
- How long will it take?
- How long will it be before we can do 'x'?

In broad terms the three main planning questions can be answered as follows:

1. We know *where we are* by looking at the recommendations of the full surveyor's report and a review of present financial liabilities and projected income. It might be expressed as follows:

    'The roof and some rainwater pipes are considered to be considerably dilapidated and need immediate action at an estimated cost of £x. We should therefore repair these immediately and hold over external redecorations for a further twelve months. Our annual income this year must include a reserve element to take account of the cost of a large contract in the coming year.'

2. We can express our intentions – *where we want to be* – by describing the building in its complete and refurbished state or the nearest approximation acceptable to the company.

    'It is our intention over a period of seven years to refurbish the whole property to as high a standard as possible by first repairing outstanding faults and then carrying out all refurbishments in accordance with the terms of the lease and then maintaining it at this level.'

3. We *get there* by planning activities (maintenance, repairs etc) and spending income (service charges and rents) methodically in a predetermined way over a period of time until the building and services reach the standard agreed in (2).

    'Our rolling plan under categories "development", "maintenance", "staff" and "amenities" contains the details of proposed action. Income will be controlled and service charge defaulters will be pursued.'

Planning

Forecasts are notoriously inaccurate. The more long-term the plan, the more likely it is to be increasingly inaccurate. Many of the assumptions

Planning strategy

that a long-term plan makes will eventually change, including those about inflation, suppliers' prices, interest rates charged by the bank, the condition of the building, and, in times of financial uncertainty, the inclination of the majority of the lessees to dig as deeply for funds as they once did. On the other hand, the shorter the plan, the less scope it has. It may prove fairly reliable over a period of twelve months, but you are dealing with a property which will almost certainly outlive its youngest resident and the proper care of which requires an altogether longer-term vision.

What is needed is a practical method which focuses in one place all objectives, with priorities for action and time-scales so that you can see (a) where you think you are, (b) where you intend to be, and (c), with all known information, how you are going to get there. In other words, you need a format which will be reliable in so far as it states your present intentions, and remains adjustable as conditions change.

One of the following three approaches to planning should meet the needs of your management company. The first is a full and detailed approach which revalues estimates on an annual basis and looks at planning on a three-year cycle. The second is the classical sinking fund and is often set up when it is contained in the terms of the lease. The third is a more pragmatic method which focuses on immediate targets on an ad hoc basis. They are:

- The rolling plan
- The reserve fund
- The project based approach.

Creating the rolling plan

The stated objectives of your company and anticipated expenses will determine the subject matter of the plan, and the headings chosen in your plan would be based upon them.

Keeping the whole thing as simple as possible, the basic formats of a rolling plan as applied to a lessee-owned block are shown in **Figure 3**. This identifies two things. First, the activities planned in successive years, which, as you build them up, become the rolling plan itself. Secondly, the estimated costs relating to those activities and expenses in each of those years.

The three main columns represent the coming year (Year 1) and the two following (Year 2 and Year 3). The descriptions of the first year's activities will be fairly accurate. Those of the second and third years can only indicate your present intentions and expected expenditure. In twelve

FIGURE 3 Model for three-year rolling plan

| | YEAR 1 || YEAR 2 || YEAR 3 ||
	Activity	Cost	Activity	Cost	Activity	Cost
DEVELOPMENT a **Refurbishments** (Five-yearly internal and external as per lease) b **Major Projects** (Rectifying major defects in the building, eg damp-proofing)						
MAINTENANCE a **Planned Maintenance** (Roofs, drains, pipes, roadways, etc) b **Maintenance Contracts** (Boilers, lifts, pest control, etc)						
PROPERTY REPAIRS Emergency maintenance and repairs						
STAFF Caretaker(s) Cleaner(s)						
AMENITIES Garages Car spaces Storage lock-ups Garden						
OTHER COSTS Insurance Electricity Sundries						
TOTALS						

months' time a new format is completed in the same way. Years 2 and 3 will become the basis of the information for Years 1 and 2, and a new Year 3 will be added. In a year's time you will be in a better position to forecast more accurately the projected activities and costs for the new Year 1.

The suggested plan has six main sections:

- Development
- Maintenance
- Property Repairs

- Staff
- Amenities
- Other Costs

It can of course use other headings, and in time you may amend it to suit your specific needs. Follow this format through and see how it compares with your own needs. Use information from your property and build up the first stage by briefly stating your objectives under each heading.

In practice you will find that most items of expenditure will remain relatively constant from year to year with the exception of the Development section, which contains Refurbishments and Major Projects. These occur at such infrequent intervals that they will vary considerably from year to year. (The sinking or reserve fund is discussed below.)

It is much easier than it seems at first. The difficulty is reconciling what needs to be done with projected income. This usually depends on what limits the company is prepared to put on service charges as the years go by. What you get from this exercise is more than a set of intentions with costs attached. You are also helping to create a measure of security for those who will have to pay, by indicating what you expect the financial position will be next year and in the two years following. Beyond that time, you are probably guessing wildly. While it is important to take a long-term view of the property and your responsibilities, a plan of this nature needs adjusting every year. The following is best illustrated by following Figure 3.

1 Development of the property

This has two sub-headings:

a Refurbishments

This refers to the continual round of painting and repairs that the landlord is required to undertake under the covenants of the lease. The two main recurring contracts are the external redecorations and repairs, often organised in a four-year cycle, and the internal redecoration of the common parts, usually in a seven-year cycle. It is not uncommon, when lessees dig deep and the funds are available, for the first external contract under a lessee-owned company to be a well-supervised and thorough one (see Chapter 11). When this is so, the company might, with the consent of the members, extend the cycle time by one or more years. The direct benefit is that the cost of the next contract is spread over a longer time and is thus less of a financial burden.

Costing will be an estimated figure based at this stage on the surveyor's estimate in his report.

However, it has been known for a leaseholder to threaten to take his lessee-owned company to court when they would not agree to authorise expenditure on external redecorations. Their four-year cycle had come round and it was the popular view that the last contract had stood up well and all might benefit if the next contract were to be held over one more year. The lessee was insistent and got his way. The work was carried out and he obtained a good price for his flat a few months later.

b Major Projects

This refers to important and urgent matters that cannot wait in the first year of ownership. It is likely that you will be concentrating on one or two major projects, and while you will have a good idea of how your plan will begin to shape up, you will not want to embark on a programme of refurbishment contracts before you are satisfied that you have done what is necessary to implement badly needed preventive remedies. These will almost certainly be hidden sources of damage to the building that have come to light as a result of the surveyor's report, such as an area of rising damp or the need to replace damaged rainwater pipes.

Costing: It is very difficult to cost future major works without obtaining quotations but this will involve paying substantial fees to the block's surveyor (see Chapter 11). However, the surveyor should be asked to provide a guestimate of the cost of future works, which they will normally give without charge against the promise of obtaining future professional work for the company.

Delaying the establishment of a formal plan during the first year while more important things are sorted out is quite common and usually meets with the full approval of all lessee/shareholders. However, it is always disappointing when the work is completed and paid for and there is little that is physically obvious to show for it. Lessees do like results and sometimes there are those who are keen to see the common parts refurbished and redecorated before all else. Beware such people: they do not necessarily have the long-term interests of the building at heart, and might just have their flats on the market. Openly drawn-up and agreed objectives usually help to avoid these problems.

However, people do want to see progress and a great deal of goodwill can be generated by undertaking as soon as possible some of the small, less expensive jobs which have been irritating people for years.

2   Maintenance

a   *Planned Maintenance*

All blocks of flats should have an established ***programme of maintenance and inspection***. Once the programme is set up, a system of management checks should be applied to it that would operate throughout the year as a matter of course. In this way, every item of plant and machinery is inspected and, where appropriate, serviced. The roofs, service pipes, rainwater drainage, waste pipes and tanks should all be subject to standard inspection and maintenance procedures. Since it is not an expensive process, its purpose being to avoid costly surprises, the long-term financial benefits to the company can be considerable (see Chapters 8 and 12).

Costing should be by an annual fixed cost. It can be identified by inviting quotes based on your surveyor's specification for the building, itemising what is to be inspected, how often and by what method each item is to be maintained.

b   *Maintenance Contracts*

Your specialist contractors will carry out maintenance on lifts, boilers, pest control and any other item or installation requiring specialist attention. However, both boilers and lifts have a life expectancy and it is imperative that you examine the terms of all your maintenance contracts and establish their expiry dates in case they are assumed to terminate with the expected useful life of the plant that is being maintained.

Costing: These costs should be identifiable from the contracts and may have a built-in increment or require your approval for any change in charges. Like any contract arrangement, it is advisable to test the market occasionally to see if you are getting value for money.

3   *Property Repairs*

Of course even in the best run block there will be unplanned emergencies that will require immediate attention.

Costing: Although unplanned, it is surprising that the annual expenditure is often very similar from one year to another so obviously past experience is the best guide. Therefore you should use the Average Annual Cost Increase by a Building Trades Price index.

4 Staff

Some residential blocks have several resident porters and a large team of daily cleaners. Others may have none or just a visiting caretaker/cleaner.

Costing: The cost of employing full-time residential staff will include wages, National Insurance, heating and lighting, materials, and any other costs they either incur as a result of the way they are required to carry out their duties or receive by way of their contracts. Once a decision is made about staffing, the costs should be predictable year on year and may only increase in line with inflation. The best way to reward outside this is with a single annual bonus (see Chapter 12).

5 Amenities

Initial expenditure on amenities is likely to be small. Unless there is a serious problem, they seem to take a low priority. Some leases allocate garages, parking spaces, gardens and storerooms as of right. In these cases there is a contractual responsibility, either on the landlord or the tenant, to keep the amenities in good repair. In other blocks the single most common cause of anxious argument is the fair allocation of car parking and other amenities (see Chapter 12).

Costing: In normal circumstances rented amenities are usually seen as a source of income rather than expenditure, so if they do constitute an unwelcome cost in the early days you may at first wish to allocate expenditure on them in line with the income they generate. Other amenities (eg roadways, lighting) that require urgent action can be costed by inviting competitive quotes from contractors to put them into good order.

6 Other Costs

There is a number of fixed and repeating costs such as block and other insurance premiums, electricity, gas and professional fees.

Costing: Your broker will tell you what your expected insurance costs are. It has been an accounting convention to increase forecast expenditure for the year ahead, but in times of low inflation more precise information may be available where annual price increases for public utilities are published before they are invoiced. Other fixed and recurring costs are usually estimated by adding a reasonable percentage to the most recently received bill.

Costs

If you have followed this through with information from your own property, you will have two pieces of information in the new plan: your projected activities/expenses over the next three years, and their estimated costs. You can now compare these with your present level of income from service charges and rents, and you will find yourself in one of three possible situations:

- Income at present levels exceeds the projected costs of your plan
- Projected costs of your plan exceed present levels of income
- They more or less balance.

While it is not uncommon for newly formed lessee companies to find themselves with loose ends (for example, a flat may not have paid service charge for some time), for the sake of simplicity it is assumed that present levels of income reflect fairly accurately the most recent service charge demands. Continuing to apply the principle that people like to know where they stand and what to expect, and that this in turn helps to facilitate consent to less agreeable but necessary decisions, you are left with some clear options:

- If more money is needed to meet expenditure, decide either to reduce expenditure or increase service charges. The advice is always to increase service charges during the honeymoon period. It is better to start with more income than less. Raising the level of service charges later suggests a lack of planning

- If income exceeds the plan's projected costs, decide whether to bring forward work from future years or set up a reserve fund. A reserve fund, sometimes called a *sinking fund*, does spread the financial burden of major contracts over a number of years. It earns interest, is seen as good management and encourages confidence. Moreover, in the absence of past experience to go on, your first year's expenditure might be higher than expected.

The outcome of these decisions gives you the start of your rolling plan. If this is updated annually as part of the routine preparations for the AGM, then you should know and be able to inform the meeting, within the bounds of acceptable human error, where you are, where you want to be and how you intend to get there – over the next year or so, anyway.

The role of planning in a lessee-owned company

Planning in a lessee-owned company is important for many reasons. Of course it is good management practice, but most lessees are very defensive about projects that affect their own living spaces and want to know that thought has been given to the peculiar features and characteristics of their building. While there are many problems that are common to most residential blocks, each has a uniqueness which must be taken into account during the planning process.

For this reason, lessee-owned companies should not copy ideas from other organisations without matching them to the specific needs, features, and peculiarities of their own membership make-up and building. The old adage 'adopt and adapt' is particularly appropriate here – especially the injunction to adapt. Each lessee-owned company develops its own personality over a period of time and no two ever seem to be the same. As events progress, time changes the company. Residents come and go, in normal circumstances at the rate of about ten per cent each year. Often a core of long-standing inhabitants, not necessarily those who get involved in the running of the building, remain. The group of decision-makers alters as the property improves and is eventually maintained to generally acceptable standards. Other and sometimes more adventurous objectives are put forward, much to the dislike of those who do not want change, or have high mortgages or fixed incomes. Thus a new and different set of arguments and objectives become the focus of debate among the lessee/shareholders and the management committee.

After six or seven years almost certainly the majority of lessee/shareholders will have forgotten what the objectives were at the outset, let alone what the problems of the building really were. People do not like to be reminded that they once lived in accommodation they themselves considered substandard. It offends polite values and they will have genuinely forgotten. There are therefore both substantive and procedural reasons why it is wise to take a systematic approach and plan in the accepted way, recording decisions and keeping a secure file of all notices, correspondence, plans, costs and drawings – not forgetting photographs. Expectations change and perceptions change with them. When you are a little crestfallen after a difficult meeting in a few years' time, the one undeniable piece of evidence will be an accurate record of where you have come from.

The reserve fund (or sinking fund)

When a resident-owned company produces new leases for its lessee/shareholders, the provision for a sinking fund is frequently written into the modernised lease. A sinking fund must be held in trust in a separate bank account from all other monies. This is usually an interest-earning deposit account. However, the contributions of an individual lessee are not returnable when a lease changes hands. This may seem unfair on a vendor who is moving out of the property. But a large and imminent maintenance expense might put off prospective buyers; indeed, without a sinking fund, the value of the flat on the market may be reduced to reflect this forthcoming cost to the purchaser. The existence of a sinking fund is, therefore, a useful selling point and if provided for in the lease, incoming lessees will be required to contribute.

The purpose of a reserve fund is to help smooth out the sharp fluctuations of service charge demand associated with cyclical expenditure on external and internal repairs and redecorations. Its primary purpose, therefore, is to benefit lessees. Its benefit to the company is that there should be less likelihood of leaseholders not being able to afford sudden and brief increases in the service charge. It is as important that the company is able to collect the service charge as it is that each lessee should feel that they are able to pay on time.

The items in the plan to which a reserve fund applies are usually *refurbishments* and might include the external and internal redecorations, roof repairs, lifts and boiler replacement. The current estimated cost of these should be known from the surveyor's report. The example used here applies to the internal and external redecorations contract only, and since the longest time between two similar contracts is assumed to be seven years, the reserve fund in this example would be operated on a seven-year cycle. Any agreed alterations to such an arrangement should be made in full knowledge of this if, for example, the period was extended.

It would be far too simple to suppose that, if the external contract were to be currently estimated at £100,000 and the internal at £40,000, it is simply a matter of dividing £140,000 by seven to give a figure of £20,000 per annum as a component of service charge to allocate to reserve. In practice, you are probably going to carry out the largest contract in sections, starting in the first year of ownership. So there is little chance now of protecting lessees from a larger than usual bill. Since the rolling plan assesses the value of the work to be carried out each year, and this forms the basis of the new calculations, then, excluding exceptional circumstances, there is no guesswork in attempting to arrive at a figure for next year's figures. The model is a simple matrix with the items down the vertical axis and the method of calculation shown on the horizontal axis (see **Figure 4**).

FIGURE 4	**A model reserve fund plan for external and internal refurbishments only (repeated annually)**						
	(1) INITIAL COST	(2) COST NOW	(3) AMOUNT COLLECTED	(4) AMOUNT OUTSTANDING	(5) YEARS LEFT	(6) COLLECT THIS YEAR
EXTERNAL REFURBS	£100.0k	£112.4k	£29.6k	£82.8k	5 of 7	£16.5k
INTERNAL REFURBS	£45.0k	£50.7k	£23.4k	£27.3k	2 of 4	£13.6k
					TOTAL	£30.1k

Column (5) 'Years left' shows that this plan was started two years ago and figures for the third year of the plan are here being prepared.

The Figures in Column (1) were estimated two years ago when the plan was set up.

Column (2) represents the estimated cost of each at today's prices. This figure should be based upon the estimated increase in building costs for the coming year. The previous two years, for the sake of example, were each estimated at 6%. This figure, then, represents the initial estimated cost, plus 6%, plus 6%. (Note: building costs do not always increase.)

Column (3) shows how much has already been collected and is held on deposit in the reserve fund. (This model does not show interest received on this money and which you may decide to take into account in these calculations.)

Column (4) is the figure you get if you subtract Column (3), the amount held in the reserve fund, from Column (2) which is today's estimated cost.

Column (6) is the figure which must be collected in the coming year and is Column (4), the amount outstanding, divided by Column (5), the number of years left.

The total, in this case £30,100, is the sum that would be apportioned between, say, fifty flats, which produces a figure in the order of £620 per flat.

The smaller the property, the more reliable this method is likely to be. In larger properties where the lease requires the landlord to supply heating and hot water, or where there are lifts, these items have a life expectancy and are the responsibility of the landlord to replace in due course. Some lessee-owned companies have tried to start reserve funds for the replacement of plant, but the figures can begin very quickly to look frighteningly large and an estimate of what something will cost in ten years' time can be wildly inaccurate. Some companies have bitten the bullet and collected over a shorter period, say two to three years, and gone ahead with boiler replacement. Others, seeing the considerable expense of the on-costs of boiler and pipework removal and replacement, with all the attendant problems associated with lagging, have faced facts and agreed to install independent boilers at a lower cost overall.

The way to use this model is to make it do what you require of it. It could include lift replacement, boiler replacement and similar requirements under the lease. The model only describes the process. In the light of what you know about your property and the policies of your company, decide which contracts you are going to include and how frequently you intend to carry them out. This information is usually obtained by having the items valued. It is well worth the cost and effort, but it is subject to the pitfalls facing any plan – namely, the unknown. But used purposefully, its benefits outweigh its liabilities. It gives you information which you would rather have at a reasonable cost than not at all, and is an attractive selling point when a flat has to be put on the market.

The project based approach

The main focus of a project based approach is the next major planned project, be it the external or internal redecorations contract, the lift replacement or boiler renewal. In practice this is the approach that is most frequently adopted as the easiest to understand and plan for. Leaseholders know what they are paying for, when it is scheduled to be done and what it is expected to cost. While it has these immediate advantages, there is an element of unfairness built in to it since a new leaseholder may arrive in the block just as a large and expensive contract is being planned. However, this method is probably the only practical approach where there is a backlog of projects.

Comparing the three approaches to planning

The rolling plan is more of a cash flow forecast with short-term and usually more accurate projections. Its main function is to be accurate and plan the management of the income and expenditure on a year-by-year basis. By contrast, the reserve fund is a long-term strategy which is based upon continually revised financial projections and eventual expenditure. The long-term nature of a reserve fund may make that idea initially unattractive to lessees and impossible to introduce immediately. The idea usually gathers momentum among lessees over a period of time as a response to the problems associated with uneven service charge demands. It is the desire to see it introduced that will help to make it work. The project based approach is a compromise which eases the financial burden by ignoring the longer-term funding problems. It is a more realistic and immediate objective and can also be made to work fairly.

ACTION

- On the basis of your agreed objectives and known costings and estimates, create a rolling plan for the forthcoming three years.
- Identify those items that should be part of a long-term financial plan and draft it in the form described.
- Estimate the annual amount that would be required to put into a reserve fund. This, or a modified form, could then become the basis of discussions about the desirability of a reserve fund.

CHAPTER 10

Lessees, subtenants and other residents: problems and solutions

This chapter explores some of the most common people problems, ranging from awkward misunderstandings to downright difficult cases. It looks at ways of dealing with a range of problems from simple but irritating breaches of covenant to continuous refusal to pay service charges. It considers the types of people who cause problems and conflicts and looks at some ways of approaching solutions. The observations here are largely drawn from experience over many years of managing residential properties in the interests of those who live in them. In order to identify discrete categories of person who have different statuses in the block, the following distinctions have been made:

- The lease uses the term *tenant* to refer to the party that has bought and owns the lease and to whom, for the sake of clarity, this book refers throughout as the *lessee* or *leaseholder*.

- The term *subtenant* is used here to refer to residents who rent from a leaseholder.

- A *resident* is someone of any legal status who lives permanently in the block and is usually eligible to belong to the residents' association.

- A *shareholder* is a leaseholder who is a member of the lessee-owned company but may or may not be a resident.

One of the most demanding and sometimes difficult aspects of being the landlord in a lessee-owned block is the management of problems arising out of relationships between people. This is partly due to the fact that those concerned are neighbours who may hold fairly strong feelings about one another. If you are a director of the company or in any way involved in taking decisions concerning the block, dealing with people requires some care and thought. The worst problems may involve others accusing you, as a director or committee member, of being insensitive and too hard in pursuing the best interests of the company. But people problems *have* to be tackled if the great majority of lessees who give constant support to the management committee are going to continue to do so.

Directors' duty of care – confused with 'caring'

A clear distinction must be made here between the benefit of the company, which is the benefit of all its shareholders (the lessees who have chosen to be members of the company), and the benefit of all residents. For much of the time these will be the same. But when they are different, the benefit of the company is paramount. This is not a matter of choice or opinion: it is a fact in law. There is often a mistaken assumption that because the company is owned by the people who live in the block, it is there to help them personally. The extreme case of this is where a cooperative ethos develops and the directors' duty of care becomes confused with 'caring' and residents begin to rely upon the company to carry out responsibilities that are properly their own. This may take the form of extra calls on the caretaker's time for small services, or, more subtly, a notion, developing into a practice, that the company carries responsibility for the security of flats (see Chapter 12).

The company does not exist to supply a social service; it is there to carry out the duties and responsibilities of the landlord as laid down in the lease. In the early days, this should be reiterated regularly so that those involved in running the company are not distracted from its proper functions. If the company does get involved in activities outside its scope of responsibilities, it may be seen to lose its impartiality and accusations of favouritism will damage its credibility when difficult residents have to be dealt with fairly.

Welfare can be the right and proper role of an active residents' association, which the well-run lessee-owned company would welcome and encourage.

The value of the 'tenant's pack'

A well-produced set of house rules (see Appendix 3) states clearly that their purpose is to protect residents from abuse, not to threaten them with sanctions. On the one hand, therefore, the company will need to make it clear that it intends to act as a prudent and responsible landlord in sorting out old problems by creating new ways of doing things; on the other, it will not want to unnerve or frighten anyone into thinking they are going to have to get rid of their pets. This is where the 'tenant's pack' comes into its own.

The tenant's pack is a small sheaf of papers in three parts which the company would normally put together initially to introduce the transitional period from old landlord- to new resident-managed block. Typically it would consist of the following.

Part 1

- A letter of welcome from the chairman with an introduction to the company and board of directors. The initial letter is a 'welcome to the company', which in due course can become a 'welcome to the block' letter for new residents.
- An extract from the Memorandum and Articles of Association, showing the main objectives and conduct of general meetings. When the business objectives have been drawn up, these might also be included.
- The structure and membership of the management committee, staircase representatives and any other appropriate information. It may also draw attention to the residents' association where one exists.

Part 2

- An abstract from the lease relating to 'tenants' covenants' with an explanation that the company is protecting the interests of those who live in and care for the block.
- A list of any 'house rules' which the directors would draw up to explain the covenants in terms of the specific needs of the block (see Appendix 3).

Part 3

- A list of 'standard conditions for contractors and conditions for seeking approval for alterations' which state clearly and firmly the circumstances under which the company as landlord will allow tenants to engage a contractor to carry out alterations or building work of any kind. It too will become part of the 'welcome pack' and is an invaluable aid to avoiding serious misunderstandings (see Appendices 2A and 2B).

As we have said elsewhere, there is no standard form for the tenants' pack; for example, some blocks include a page on useful information and telephone numbers. Since the purpose of this is to do a regulating and communicating job, the best advice is to fit the contents of your pack to the specific needs of your particular building.

In this way, the company's intended policy on tackling long-term abuses of tenancies can be eased into action. It may be necessary to do some persuading, especially with the less adaptable resident, but, with a light touch, conformity can be achieved by agreeing temporary exceptions with time limits. For example, there may be residents who rely on pets for company and who have not been asked to remove them from the premises by the previous landlord. They might well be allowed to keep them so long as they are properly cared for and do not cause a nuisance of any kind. However, in the interests of hygiene, no new pets would be introduced into the block from the present date.

Rules should be drafted to encourage agreeable behaviour rather than to penalise disagreeable behaviour – the lease already does that for you. Not only should you start off as you mean to go on, but, once set, the standards must be seen to be monitored, maintained and repeatedly explained. For example, some leases permit the keeping of pets, usually on the basis of a revocable licence granted by the landlord, while others forbid them in the building. In each case, the lease provides the guidelines.

The early days are a time to explain rather than impose. Residents who subsequently create problems will not get much sympathy if they have been given all the normal courtesies when matters are first explained.

Abuse of leases by leaseholders

The unintentional offender

Most people at one time or another will have been unwittingly in breach of their leases. They might, for example, have been noisy, kept objectionable pets or abused or overused the common parts in some way. Up until now, such breaches have probably been either put up with or ignored because the old landlord has been unwilling to get involved, regardless of how troublesome the breach of covenant has been. However, the company retains the right to require all residents to keep the tenants' covenants in the lease. In addition, the lease usually permits the landlord to make additional reasonable rules.

Often the most insignificant aspects of anti-social behaviour are those which most annoy the ordinary rule-abiding resident. For example, the neighbour who leaves his rubbish out on the one day in the week when there is no scheduled collection, coinciding with the monthly dinner party in the flat opposite. Or the pram constantly parked haphazardly at the bottom of the stairway obstructing the only fire escape.

It is surprising how very amenable, understanding and cooperative culprits can be. We have all been in a position where we have certainly had no desire to offend, and being guilty of something, have had to apologise profusely. After such an episode or misunderstanding, acquaintances often become friends, and when the instance is referred to later it is generally done so with good humour. The first rule is avoid the stand-off, the abrupt note pinned to the rubbish sack thanking them for their thoughtlessness. Avoid anything that might be resented later. One useful approach is to use a circular to all residents about the problem so as not to focus on one person. But always be prepared to talk and assume that most reasonable people respond reasonably when approached in the right way at the right time – and the right time is usually when the other person is not preoccupied with what they perceive as something more important.

Sometimes an older person may become confused or simply forgetful. Old people are seldom stupid and more often than not they have someone special to whom they go for help and advice, a family 'minder', be they an old family friend, or a favourite nephew. If this is not the case, their regular confidante could be a member of the residents' association or a close neighbour. Whoever that is, involve them and keep that person informed and helpful in informing any older person who has not entirely understood the changes that are taking place. The last thing you want is a difficult stand-off with one of the oldest and most revered residents you have. Everyone in the building has dealt with the previous landlord, so they should be used to the dealing with the new one, no matter how young or old the leaseholder. But the change in ownership, and its consequences, may need explaining to some people through a third party in order to ensure that life goes on as normal.

This is a further reason, especially in larger blocks, for supporting a residents' association and seeking its cooperation and why some companies circulate an annual reminder of the 'house rules' to all residents (see below and Appendix 3). These would obviously include reference to the simple day-to-day matters which have caused the most complaint, such as when to put out rubbish, the use and abuse of common parts, responsibility for security, the use of caretaker's time and so forth.

More difficult leaseholders

Enforcing rules on other residents – usually their own neighbours – is one of the most difficult tasks for directors of lessee-owned companies. This is especially true where there are repeated, and intentional, breaches of the terms of lease. This sort of problem can give rise to much heart-searching by directors, committee members and shareholders, since no one wants to take on the mantle of the heavy-handed landlord.

On the other hand, why on earth should a lessee be allowed to continue to behave in an anti-social way to the annoyance of everybody? If one resident is allowed to get away with it, why should anybody keep the rules? The wilful abuse of a lease is very often seen as an abuse of those leaseholders who have put considerable personal effort into ensuring that the block is purchased and the management company set up to the benefit of all resident leaseholders. Adding insult to injury, the offending resident(s) may at that time have been openly critical of the whole exercise.

There is therefore really very little to worry the conscience about here. Shared responsibility is an integral part of the ethos of lessee-owned companies and experience has shown that boards of directors of resident-owned companies are very much tougher on blatant breaches of lease than the average traditional landlord. Instead of receiving the increasingly insistent three reminders he was used to under the old landlord, the lessee who buys a new car, has his flat redecorated or goes on an expensive holiday about the time when he receives (and for the third time ignores) his service charge demand, has been known under the new regime, to get one reminder followed shortly by a writ. The reason is simple. While his attitude may, for obvious reasons, have been understandable and consistent with that of other residents under the previous landlord, the same behaviour is now deemed selfish, inappropriate and deeply offensive to members of the new lessee-owned company.

The ultimate sanction a landlord has under the lease, where lessees are in breach of lease – whether it be changing the internal structure of the flat without permission and refusing to reinstate, or persistently abusing an eleven o'clock rule about excessive noise at night – is the **Section 146 Notice** and the threat of *forfeiture*. (This is discussed in more detail below under 'Bad payers and non-payers' and 'Forfeiture'.) Again, take care to ensure that the company has acted fairly and reasonably to settle the matter *before* instructing the solicitor to issue the Notice. But in the instance of persistent breach of covenant, unlike a case of an unpaid service charge, the lessee usually becomes automatically liable to pay the landlord's costs from the moment the solicitor is instructed.

In theory, the problem leaseholder could forfeit his lease, although, in practice, a judge will normally do everything possible to prevent this from happening so that the person is not made homeless. The worst possible outcome would only occur if the lessee either continues to ignore the company's requests to rectify the problem or otherwise continues to act in a completely irresponsible manner. If the lessee has been clearly informed of their position within the terms of the lease, and you have taken action to protect the interests of the company, then any penalty incurred by the leaseholder is of their own making. In which case the company may end up owning the flat in question and rectifying the problem itself.

Difficulties of this nature are often inherited problems, and whether you like it or not, the perennial anti-authoritarian is now going to confer on to your company the worst attributes of 'the bad landlord'. Acting lawfully and quickly pacifies the understandable feelings of injustice and anger other leaseholders have expressed who themselves have been content to give their time and effort in the common interest, and have been happy to pay their fair share.

Abuse of lease by subtenants

Leaseholders let their flats to subtenants for two main reasons:

- So that the flat does not stand empty
- To make money from the property while they themselves are not using it – so that the property pays for itself.

The lease is the contract between the management company and the non-resident lessee (the person letting the flat). The non-resident lessee has, or should have, a tenancy agreement with the subtenant requiring the subtenant to keep the lessees' covenants in the lease. This may not be so in every instance when you first take over the management. But where it is possible to apply, no lessee should sublet without the permission of the landlord. This is so that agreements between absentee lessees and their subtenants can be vetted by the company and checked to ensure that renting subtenants are aware of the terms under which the lessee owns the flat.

It follows that if a subtenant is in constant abuse of the tenants' covenants, and does not respond to reasonable requests to conform, then the company can approach the lessee who owns the flat, and in the first instance inform him of the nature of the complaint. He may after all be oblivious of the whole matter. Further, he should be told that if the resident of his flat continues to be in breach of the lease, the company will require him to remove the resident. If this proves ineffective, a threat of action against the lessee under Section 146 of the Law of Property Act 1925 (see below). Adopting the fair, reasonable and direct approach usually acts as sufficient motivation for the lessee to get legal advice, which resolves the problem.

Solicitors will often suggest some sort of compromise as a reasonable course of action, and you might, for good reasons, find this attractive. But beware: the solicitor is not responsible for managing the company and, through it, the property. Neither does he have to answer criticisms from your shareholders such as, 'Why doesn't the company hurry up and stop these subtenants disrupting our lives?' A solicitor's job is to take your instructions and advise you to the best of his ability as to your position in law. He may have had absolutely no experience of management whatsoever, and in accepting advice that makes good sense to him, you could find yourself responsible for the continuing outcome of half measures. In difficult cases, always be prepared to be fair and be firm within the law. You will have to make decisions distasteful to yourself and apparently autocratic and insensitive to others only if the offending party forces you to do so.

Some local authorities take the problems of neighbour nuisance very seriously. Anti-social behaviour, noise and other nuisances may warrant the attention of the police. The council or the police can apply for an order to the magistrates' court to protect people from anti-social behaviour. A breach of an order is a criminal offence and the consequences can be severe. It is also useful to keep to hand the telephone number of the local authority's department of environmental services who can serve notices for a range of nuisances.

Buy to let – rent for profit

Recent years have seen a substantial increase in *buy to let* purchases within residential blocks. After all, as long as the flat pays for itself, the new absentee lessee does not have to bother about safeguarding his investment; you are going to do that for him. So buy to let has introduced to the flat-dwelling market a new type of resident-occupied flat. In particular, they can be identified as flats that:

- Are owned and let primarily for profit.
- Have a more frequent turnover of occupants.
- Are more likely in breach of the multi-occupancy clause in the lease.
- Contain young professional couples or groups, rather than families.
- Have absentee leaseholders who have not lived in the block.

In fact *buy to let* refers to the event when the flat was purchased. ***Rent for profit*** is the continuing relationship the absentee leaseholder has with the resident management company. The effect of rent for profit can be, and certainly has been, directly at odds with the ethos and objectives of resident-owned and managed companies, which have been specifically created to preserve the long-term interests of the building and its lessee/shareholders.

The ***renting subtenants*** who typify this new flat-dwelling resident, and who account in some instances for one-tenth of occupancy, can be generally described as people who:

- Are young professionals.
- Are attracted to large flats where rents can be shared between many people.
- Prefer more rooms, all of which can be used as individual bedrooms and let individually.
- Have lifestyles substantially different from the majority of residents.
- Have no formal contact with or direct contract between themselves and the resident-owned company.
- Pay rent to their landlord (the absentee lessee) who has little knowledge or experience of life in the block itself.

This is a recipe for a catalogue of complete misunderstanding. You can lessen the impact by informing the flat-owner of the company's existence and his responsibilities under the lease, thus holding him responsible for the actions of his subtenants and any breaches of covenant. Give him a set of house rules at the outset to give to his subtenants. From here on always act reasonably towards the new residents and never put yourself in a position where you can be accused of victimisation. If other residents are causing similar problems, treat them all the same at the same time.

If you receive a number of reasonable and serious complaints about the occupancy of a sublet flat and these are breaches of the tenants' covenants in the lease, write to the absentee leaseholder giving details of the breaches with the times and dates. The matter needs to be a serious and continuing breach; one complaint is usually insufficient to impress a court. Repeat the process if you receive complaints about a second serious breach of covenant. On the third occasion write to the absentee leaseholder, show that there have been many complaints and that you are being very reasonable concerning the offending subtenants and ask him if he admits the breach of lease (see 'Forfeiture' below). Explain to him the course of action open to you, first an application to the Leasehold Valuation Tribunal and then, if the matter remains unresolved, to the court for forfeiture. If he takes legal advice and discovers his vulnerability, that, given the balance of probabilities, usually resolves the matter. It has cost you time and trouble, he keeps his flat and you should find you get nice, quiet and friendly subtenants living there from then on.

But you have to start at the first complaint, be very purposeful and be able to show that at all times you have been reasonable. If you let up, you lose it. If you see it through, it's much easier next time.

New residents

New leaseholders, those who arrive after the takeover by the lessees, will have no notion of the time and effort you and others put in to running the company and the many decisions that have been made along the way. They just feel very pleased they found a nice flat in a block where everyone seems so keen and involved. The fact that the building is owned by its lessees will for some time be an incentive for new people to buy in when flats become available on the market. It may marginally affect the value of the flats, especially where there are neighbouring blocks which are not self-managed and that it is apparent that the lessee-owned company has made noticeable improvements to its property. An enterprising new lessee can find himself on the board of directors in a few years and will be able to influence policy and the future of the block.

However, new, 'post-buyout' leaseholders will not have lived through the freehold purchase or the setting up of the management company with the other active lessees in the block and their perceptions and expectations will probably be different. They will have come into the block having done their sums and at a time when there is no sense of uncertainty about the future of the building. The importance of clearly stated business objectives has been discussed previously, but this is an instance where their repetition and review for the sake of clarity is useful. New lessees and especially new directors should be put in the picture as to why the block was bought and what the agreed business plan is.

Concerning alterations to flats

New residents, whether lessees or subtenants, do what everybody does when they move into a new home. So as to stamp their personality on their new flat, they decide how they are going to get it just as they want it. They will decide on colour schemes for various rooms, what sort of cooker to install, where they want the washing machine and dishwasher. Some are more adventurous and will want to change the use of certain rooms, add a bathroom or extend an area of living space by removing a wall or two. It is likely that they bought the flat with the full expectation that they would be able to make these changes.

Whether or not it is possible to get the appropriate 'welcome pack' to incoming lessees *before* they arrive, rather than later when they have taken up residence in the building, the company's authority on the issue of internal modifications must be asserted at the outset. Make sure the new lessee has a copy of the company's 'Building works and the refurbishment of flats' and 'Standard Conditions for Contractors' (see

Appendices 2A and 2B) and ensure in the most polite yet firm way that they are adhered to. This will almost certainly require the new leaseholder to pay the cost of the company's surveyor to advise and inspect the works in the normal professional manner. The alternative is to risk damage to the structure of the building which may affect a number of adjacent flats, or other problems which can arise as a result of apparently innocuous changes to structures being left in the hands of people new to flat-dwelling.

The problem of controlling both new and existing residents who wish to make substantial changes to their flats, and who are also your own neighbours, is one which needs an understanding but very firm hand. Appendices 2A and 2B spell out in detail conditions that have been used as management tools by experienced resident-owned companies. They may need to be adapted to your own needs but come strongly recommended.

Case study 1

In a North London block, the lessee of a top-floor flat removed his chimney breast and flue to give his sitting-room more space. Some months later, the resident below tried to light a fire and smoke poured into the flat above. Although the top-floor alteration was eventually reinstated at some cost and a surveyor was sued for negligence, the whole affair involved the participation of a new surveyor, a structural engineer, the local authority and their respective lawyers, who earned fat fees in the process.

Case study 2

The small service lift shafts found on the corner of large blocks are called 'dumb waiters'. A new tenant in a fourth-floor flat had engaged an eager one-man outfit to install his new kitchen. The man advised the tenant to get rid of the dumb waiter in the kitchen, since it was no longer used and by so doing he would gain more kitchen and therefore more cooking space. The tenant agreed to this, together with the appropriate adjustment in the price of the job (which is why the builder proposed the demolition of the dumb waiter in the first place). Being on the top floor, all the winding gear for the now defunct mechanism had to be removed as well. In the process, the man sent most of the tackle and about a dozen house bricks down the empty shaft, crashing on to the top of the ground-floor tenant's washing machine. He, in turn, had been told previously that this space in his flat was redundant and could be put to good use by installing an appliance in it.

> The first the new top-floor resident knew was when the ground-floor recipient of the bricks and cable, ignoring fears for his heart condition, was found beating on the door of the top flat in a state of semi-collapse, having rushed up the eight flights of stairs separating their front doors. It is said that apologies were profuse and the new man did what he could to make amends. But when the ground-floor resident had a further heart attack and widowed his wife some months later, the new top-floor tenant felt a strange pang of guilt.

Drainage

The drainage systems of older blocks were not designed for modern appliances and their extensive use. This applies particularly to the installation of additional bathrooms, dishwashers and some waste disposal units that are fitted to modern sinks. Some buildings have already outgrown their capacity to drain all domestic waste effectively, simply because there has been no control over the installation of new equipment.

New residents should be made aware of these problems, and if the company has already got a policy for increasing drainage capacity and design, it may be appropriate to require the new lessee to contribute to the installation of additional capacity if it is required.

Communality vs privacy

The staircase representatives in large blocks, or the director with responsibilities for residents in smaller buildings, play an important role in getting the newcomer to understand the rules of the block. New residents do not intentionally go out of their way to upset or offend and break the rules. No one wants to get off on the wrong foot. Neither do people want to think that they have somehow joined a terribly jolly bunch of flat-dwellers who live in one another's pockets. People want their privacy, and in fact this unwritten rule seems to be one of the most adhered to of all among people who live in flats. It is as though living in such close proximity, and despite sharing common parts and services, and the sounds and smells of domestic life they give rise to, people who live in blocks of flats are remarkably observant of privacy – mainly their own.

The fine point of balance for the company is where to assert itself as an active landlord protecting its position and acting in its own interests, and where to leave the resident alone to enjoy his lawful pursuits within his own walls. But you are not starting at square one. After all, most people in the building will be well acquainted with town life and flat-dwelling. This, then, means either that those who offend do so unwittingly, because they are new to the life, or that they are experienced, difficult and all the more culpable for it.

Responding to disputes between leaseholders

In some leases, tenants' covenants are ***not mutually enforceable***. This means that the lessee-owned company, being the landlord, cannot be required by a leaseholder to instruct another resident to keep the covenants of the lease. The company may, therefore, find that it can use its own discretion as to whether or not it intends to enforce covenants when asked to by an offended party.

New lessee-owned companies, for example, of smaller blocks, without a history of difficult tenancies, may not want to get involved in inter-flat disputes. In this case a lessee will have no recourse to the landlord to insist that another resident conforms to the tenants' covenants and will have to take up the case himself.

But for reasons of good management and control, some companies will give a high priority, if the lease does not already contain it, to the introduction of ***mutually enforceable covenants*** and make a point of including this provision when making variations to new leases (see Chapter 6).

If in the existing leases, covenants are not mutually enforceable, some leaseholders, because previously disputes have gone unresolved, might see the adoption of the new provision of mutually enforceable covenants as an opportunity to put pressure on directors in order to try to make sure they do enforce covenants. The answer is to make clear to everybody from the outset that there will be a short transitional period during which the company will be able to remind everybody what the covenants and house rules are and how it intends to apply them. It would also be a good time to explain the question of ***security of cost***.

Security of cost

If a resident complains to the company, asking it to take action against another lessee who is in breach of covenant, and covenants *are* mutually enforceable under the lease, the company must take action to ensure the offending party remedies the default. But it is to the complaining lessee that the company should apply to pay the company's costs for resolving the problem on their behalf. This should be agreed between the company and the complaining lessee before any action is taken. The lease may require that some, if not all, of the costs are recoverable from the offending party: in this case a refund will be made by the company to the complaining party.

This approach may seem unfair, but it is underpinned by a solid rationale. The landlord cannot incur costs on behalf of all the lessees in respect of a dispute between two particular individuals.

Serious problems and difficult cases

The most serious and difficult cases are often the easiest to understand. The thing that makes them difficult are the people involved, their unreasonableness, intransigence or downright stupidity which in turn fuels the issue and keeps the problem alive. The company's job is to apply the lease with fairness, impartiality and reasonableness. This is the virtue of a well-prepared tenant's pack which the company will be issuing to all residents, not just the difficult ones.

Bad payers and non-payers

The most effective sanction available to a landlord (the resident-owned company), in the case of non-payment of service charge by a leaseholder, is the issue through a solicitor of a Section 146 Notice for forfeiture (see section on forfeiture below). This cannot be issued until the matter of the unpaid service charge has been admitted by the leaseholder, or deemed to both exist and be reasonable by the Leasehold Valuation Tribunal. Even before that is a consideration, there are the normal, reasonable and businesslike steps that can be taken to settle the matter in a friendly manner.

Most lessee-owned companies will, at one time or another, face the problem of late payment of service charges. Some will have to deal with refusal to pay. Late payment is frequently due to forgetfulness or a temporary inability to pay and will be quite swiftly and amicably resolved. The deliberate withholding of payment is another matter altogether. At best, this behaviour is insensitive, and at worst, potentially damaging to the company and life in general because it upsets people who do pay promptly.

Whether you have a only a few non-payers in the block, or there is a long history of non-payment of service charge generally, a policy which follows up all unpaid service charges with a reminder after two weeks is adequate to begin what should be a businesslike and swift series of standard letters.

The standard system frequently adopted in chasing unpaid service charges is to send three reminders. If there is no admission of the debt or reply from the leaseholder, an application to the Leasehold Valuation Tribunal would be made to determine the matter with a view to issuing a Section 146 Notice. Initial letters are usually spaced two or three weeks apart, in order to establish that the leaseholder agrees that he owes the sum charged and will pay, or has an objection to paying it. Blocks that have managing agents usually prefer to leave the matter in their hands because of the sensitive nature of the problem. But lessee-owned companies who manage their own affairs need to address the whole matter of bad payers as soon as possible.

Since the worst outcome of non-payment of service charge is litigation leading to forfeiture (see below) the company must act fairly, reasonably and responsibly in attempting to obtain payment. There is no need at this stage to instruct a solicitor unless you do not have the time to keep close control on matters (and then you will need to keep close control on, and contact with, the solicitor).

In precise terms, you need to follow a course of action that a tribunal would accept as being fair and reasonable if the case came before it. This approach is more likely to get the matter settled quickly 'out of court', because the non-paying lessee will realise, if he takes advice, that you have adopted the appearance of a determined and correct path to litigation. The one thing you can use here to the company's benefit is reasonable urgency in keeping the process moving along.

Under no circumstances should you single out one person as an example, unless there is only one person involved. Then you should make sure that your accounts record clearly, at a particular date, how all service charge accounts stand so that you can show that this case is a genuine exception. Singling out one person for special treatment is victimisation. Regardless of the feelings of the other lessees – and there is often a great deal of pressure from those who reasonably believe that their prompt payment is subsidising the bad payer – a tribunal or court would not look kindly on this sort of approach and the non-payer will know this and milk it for all it is worth.

The sequence of formal letters

The first reminder would be a simple circular letter to all leaseholders whose service charges remain unpaid.

Another two to three weeks later, if service charges remain unpaid, follow up with a second reminder, which will contain or refer to the following items:

- A copy of the initial service charge demand.
- The date of the previous reminder letter.
- A reference to that part of the lease which requires lessees to pay service charges.
- The consequences of non-payment, giving a clear and reasonable time limit.

If the two letters remain unanswered and the service charge unpaid, you can assume you have a problem. The Leasehold Valuation Tribunal will want to decide whether the amount is owed and if it is reasonable. The third letter should therefore request this information and state the intention of the company to apply to the Leasehold Valuation Tribunal. Thus, the final letter requesting payment should:

- Refer to the two previous letters by date.
- Request that the leaseholder acknowledges the amount of the arrears.
- Request a reason for non-payment.

Part of the skill in sending letters of this nature involves not only getting the content right but also avoiding the most frequent mistakes people make in sending them. Bear in mind the following rules about issuing letters requesting payment of service charges:

- All letters of this type coming from the company should be as impersonal as possible.
- Send the correspondence to the lessee's private address, unless requested in writing to send it to a different address.
- Use a sealed envelope; an unsealed or open letter of this type read by a third party, such as a work colleague or flatmate, may be construed as defamatory.
- Do *not* mark the letter 'without prejudice' – writing 'without prejudice' on the letter would usually exclude its content from being used as evidence in a court of law.
- Avoid the spectacle of residents lurking around front doors witnessing the hand delivery of a company letter. It may be a secure and

inexpensive way of establishing delivery, but no matter how impartially carried out, it can create a distraction if allegations of personal involvement are made later. Always send an important letter of this type by post and, if thought necessary, by recorded delivery.

Some companies much prefer letters to be written by a solicitor, who would handle the case from this point on because it may require an application to a Leasehold Valuation Tribunal and ultimately the issuing of a Section 146 Notice both of which require a familiarity with the administration involved. However, two important matters will have been established by now:

- First, directors can report these events to lessee/shareholder meetings, without naming parties, and leaseholders will be clear that the company takes prompt action in these matters. Any notion that a persistent non-payer is getting away with it will be laid to rest.
- Secondly, the basis of a sound case will have been laid, so that if it gets as far as a tribunal hearing, the company will be in a strong position. Remember that the directors, in instructing this course of action, have always to act in the interests of the company. It is the company as a corporate legal entity that is taking this action, not the people involved in running it.

If there is any approach from the non-payer during these preliminaries, always remember that legal advice usually warns that part payment should not be accepted because the company may then be seen as accepting the changed situation which will compromise its initial legal position. Having only received a proportion of the debt, the company would not be able to sue for forfeiture until the next demand went unpaid.

The directors may be asked, or required, to take a view on what, under the circumstances and in the interests of the company, would be a fair and reasonable delay in proceedings, in order to allow the non-payer to find the appropriate funds. If conceded by the company and then abused by the leaseholder, the company may decide to ignore further requests and go ahead with obtaining a date for a court hearing.

If the non-payer is simply a feckless person who has the money and does not answer letters, you can judge whether you are likely to get payment at some stage in the proceedings before the case actually gets to court. However, the worst case may be an absentee lessee or someone who is adamant that they will not or cannot pay. The 'will not pay' person may end up in court paying both their and your costs unless a friend strongly advises them to act sensibly in their own interests and pay up.

On the other hand, the persistent non-payer may be a 'cannot pay' person. Again, your responsibility to the interests of the company is paramount. Few people arrive at the 'can't pay' stage overnight. They will have a number of possible sources of assistance. No matter how deserving or unfortunate the individual non-payer has been, you may not make an undertaking which commits the company to a course of action without a full discussion and decision by the board of directors.

Forfeiture

Each lessee has signed a lease and has an obligation under it to handle his affairs in a responsible manner. Currently, the company's ultimate sanction against a lessee who ignores service charge demands, and will not pay, is to instigate proceedings for *forfeiture*. In other words, the company seeks to obtain possession of the flat itself, so that the lessee forfeits the lease. This can only be done if the Leasehold Valuation Tribunal has first decided that the unpaid service charge exists and is reasonable. The Notice itself must be prepared by the company's solicitor.

This is a contentious subject because the threat of forfeiture has in the past been abused by some private landlords in order to obtain possession of flats by allowing leaseholders unknowingly to be in breach of their own leases. Recent legislation has attempted to rectify this and in the process has created a number of stages that all landlords, including resident-owned companies, must now follow in order to claim unpaid service charges through the threat of forfeiture. In general terms the steps are as follows and each assumes that the matter has not been resolved at a previous stage:

1 Direct correspondence with the leaseholder to ask them to confirm that they have an objection to the service charge and if that objection is based upon the reasonableness of the amount or the object of the expenditure.

2 An application to the Leasehold Valuation Tribunal for a hearing which will determine whether the service charge debt exists and that it is reasonable.

3 Instruction to the company's solicitor to issue a Notice under Section 146 of the Law of Property Act 1925 for forfeiture.

4 Application to the court for a judgement.

Because this process might take some time and the Tribunal would come to a decision which might be accepted in a court of law, it is unlikely now that a case would end up in court unless the leaseholder ignored the process altogether or if one of the parties was unreasonably obstinate.

In the event that it does go to court, forfeiture must be heard before a judge and would not therefore be the subject of a small claims case. In cases where unpaid amounts of £350 or less are involved, the more appropriate route would be the Small Claims Court.

In the past, judges have been disinclined, in the first instance, to turn people out of their homes and this has been a source of protection for the lessee at this stage. But it remains to be seen whether this measure of indulgence will remain the norm at the end of a longer process, following a decision of the Leasehold Valuation Tribunal in favour of the resident management company.

Experience has shown that the need for an effective sanction of this order is essential if a lessee-owned company is going to be able to exercise authority consistent with the responsibilities it carries. For the company itself, the long-term problem is not the bad payer, it is the good leaseholder who has paid up and has supported the company and feels aggrieved if nothing is done about the service charge defaulters he is effectively subsidising. If the company is unable to act quickly and effectively within the law, the great danger is that it will lose the confidence of its supporters. The added safeguard for the leaseholder of a Leasehold Valuation Tribunal hearing, before action for forfeiture can be initiated, adds to the time it will take to resolve a non-payment problem. This will require patience by the 'paid up' leaseholders who believe that the service charge was reasonable from the outset. Because forfeiture can only be administered and applied for through a solicitor and then the courts, it is unlikely to be the result of a capricious or vindictive act by a resident-owned company.

Financial leverage against bad payers

There are some entirely lawful, expedient and virtually costless methods of chasing bad payers.

There is an obligation on the landlord, when considering suing a lessee to reclaim unpaid service charges, before going to court, to check the details of the property at the Land Registry. This will ensure that all those who have a financial interest in the property, such as a building society or a bank, can be informed.

As it is in the company's interests to achieve a quick and inexpensive outcome to problems of non-payment, informing a mortgage company that one of its members is in default is an inexpensive way of bringing substantial pressure to bear on the lessee to pay up promptly. Building societies usually act swiftly to ensure that their investments are safe and secure, but will not at this stage make a payment themselves. The practice of informing the building society under these circumstances is now a well-established one.

It would be considered defamatory to publish a list of service charge non-payers within the block in order to bring pressure through embarrassment. The Annual General Meeting, however, provides an opportunity for shareholders to request details of financial information from the company directors. This information could include a list of the company's debtors. If this request is a genuine attempt by shareholders to obtain company information to which they are entitled, revealing such a list, though a very sensitive matter, is thought not to constitute a defamatory act. It has been known to be an effective method in prompting people to pay on time – so as not to appear on next year's list. But first get a legal opinion as to how, in your company, it might be handled.

Hardship cases

Hardship cases, when a leaseholder cannot pay because their personal financial circumstances constitute genuine hardship, pose very difficult problems. This might be caused by a recent loss of job, a marriage break-up or simply the fact that a resident's fixed pension is inadequate. These should be, and usually are, handled with sympathy and compassion and as much confidentiality as possible, remembering at all times to allow the person the dignity of acting on advice – rather than forcing them into a particular course of action.

Nonetheless, in fairness to all other service charge payers, a way must be found to settle the debt. This may involve the lessee asking you to provide sensitive information concerning unpaid service charge in confidence to the social services. If as a last resort the lessee has to sell their flat, your first responsibility is to the company and you will need to claim the debt from the sale of the flat. A proper way of dealing with this would be, as the freeholder, to give the information to the purchaser's solicitor, in the normal course of supplying replies to his property search, namely that there is some outstanding service charge payable on the flat.

An interesting case may be where a leaseholder accepts, in writing, that the service charge demands are correct and due for payment. It is then possible for the company, as landlord, to go straight to forfeiture (not via the LVT) at which point the mortgage lender will pay outstanding service charges, even if previously they have refused to lend extra money to the borrower!

Conflict

While most blocks will contain perfectly agreeable and harmless eccentrics upon whom the obligatory complainers can focus their attentions, some residential blocks will have many long-term unresolved conflicts among its residents. It is useful to look at some of the causes of both obvious and hidden conflicts. This is especially helpful in larger blocks – those that we have identified as Types A and C.

The following examples are, of course, stereotypes, but they help to illustrate the sources of conflict. They may be found in any grouping of lessees, regardless of the size of the building.

- The young couple who have been in the block for two years, are repaying a high mortgage, prefer a lower service charge, and are therefore looking to a period of some years to bring the building up to standard.

- The resident of many years' standing who has seen it all and is now in late middle age, with a small mortgage or none at all, and who has been waiting longingly for the day when the lessees own the block so that all the wrongs can be put right. He is prepared to pay his full share of a substantial service charge to make sure the rest of his days are agreeable.

- The very old widow on a fixed income who is worried about changes she does not fully understand, cannot move to another place (and, indeed, why should she?), and is 'looked after' by an old family friend who visits her occasionally as well as the dreaded nephew who will inherit.

- The family who rent one of the leased-back flats which is still owned by the previous landlord, have done so for the past fifteen years, and who now see themselves as second-class residents because they cannot join the company as they do not own their flat. The family is well known in the block through its three musical teenage children, dog, cat, and drum kit.

- The three sibling flat-sharers who live in the 'family trust flat', work variously for a West End auction house, a merchant bank and a bi-monthly society magazine, throw marvellous parties from which residents get respite when the trio goes to Switzerland in January to ski, the West Indies in March for some sun and Scotland for a fortnight in August, and whose understanding of, and interest in, the company is very limited.

> • The recently redundant manager scraping around for some consultancy, hoarding his severance pay against an even rainier day, who did most of the initial work on the freehold buyout and was one of the first named directors of the lessee-owned company.

The most obvious conflicts occur because people have different sets of expectations about (a) money, or what is to be considered priority expenditure, and (b) social values, or what is to be considered acceptable neighbourly behaviour.

In the first type of conflict three main conflicting points of view often emerge:

- Those who wish to improve the property in the short term and who are presently able to contribute towards the necessary works.
- Those who share the wish to improve the property but who cannot afford any immediate works and who want to take a longer-term approach to major improvements.
- A minority who have little if any concern for the future of the property and simply want a bare minimum of expenditure until they move on in two years' time or so.

In the first two cases at least, each resident cares as much for the block as the other. Their differences arise out of their different circumstances, and these are matters which are not normally openly discussed.

The second type of conflict, about social values, is really one of manners. It can be thought of as being between those who believe that neighbourly behaviour lies somewhere between a strict adherence to the tenants' covenants and common sense, and those that have never given it a thought. These conflicts usually hang on a perceived or actual breach of covenant combined with a complete insensitivity to, or ignorance of, the other's point of view.

Should the company get involved?

The terms of the lease provide the best guidance in deciding whether a conflict is one in which the company should get involved. In all but the most exceptional of cases, the company has no business trying to resolve conflicts where there is no breach of the terms of the lease, however compelling the circumstances might seem. There will be many instances where the heart dictates one course of action but where cool reflection will tell you that it is outside the terms of reference of the company. When the company does need to get involved and is, for example, required to apply a mutually enforceable covenant, then the usual rules apply, as does security of cost (see above).

Constructive conflict

Interestingly, conflict can be a positive influence which might be used as a vehicle to generate activity to solve problems. This is the very nature of robust debate. There is nothing very much wrong with healthy conflict between mature adults when both sides ultimately accept a code of practice and joint responsibility for committee decisions. Under these sometimes very productive and well-intentioned circumstances, there is nothing worse than the intervention of the 'peacemaker' who cannot himself handle open argument. Confusing conflict with confrontation, he does everything he can to prevent the two opposing sides of the argument being properly expressed, thus stifling the possibility of finding a mutually agreeable solution.

Compromise vs collaboration

Compromise is a difficult notion when conflict is acute. Collaboration is better and different. Because there is always a bigger enemy to each than the other – and this may be the prospect of losing a considerable benefit – the loss of that benefit should be made the focus of attention for both parties. When both parties may want action but at different speeds, stalemate can be worse than either, reducing the company to inactivity. This causes a hidden expense in continued deterioration of fabric or rising prices.

Parties do not have to agree in order to collaborate, and working together does make for a better understanding between opposing sets of people. Many a conflict has benefited from placing opposing parties in a working group, such as a sub-committee, and giving them something entirely unconnected with their differences to deal with, especially when there has been a particularly difficult problem to solve. The benefits of learning about the way the other sees problems and goes about tackling difficult matters, often seeps into the initial conflict with calming, if not resolving, effects. But then again it can all go terribly wrong, depending upon the maturity of the parties involved.

Where two conflicting, genuine and honest opinions are held, and where that conflict is liable to escalate until it affects the interests of the company, the company becomes a party to the conflict, however unwilling. It is then the duty of the directors to enforce a solution: either the authority of the company must be imposed or correct legal action should be taken. And this may even result in a member leaving the block.

ACTION

- Construct a 'welcome pack' with introductory letter, copy of tenants' covenants, 'house rules' and 'builders' conditions'.
- Decide upon a suing policy with the appropriate texts of standard letters:
    - how many letters
    - how spaced
    - contents
    - how delivered
    - decide which solicitor you would use for suing.
- Check with your local authority to see what assistance you can get in dealing with nuisance.
- Obtain relevant literature.

READING

LEASE, *The Leasehold Valuation Tribunal – a user's guide* – free booklet.

LEASE, *Service Charges, Ground Rent and Forfeiture* – free booklet.

CHAPTER 11

Building contracts and specifications

The lease will require the block to be redecorated every five years or so. This procedure, possibly subject to delays in the past, serves the dual function of keeping the building looking good and providing an opportunity for regular inspection. Unless nothing is considered more urgent, this is usually the first major activity a new resident company undertakes.

No company embarks on major works of this kind without a legal written contract. A building contract is a specialised document. Because it is being prepared for a particular building, it needs to be drawn up by a professional so that the company has the greatest possible protection and the contractor the most opportunity to carry out the contract. A good contract will be well balanced to protect both parties: one from substandard work, and the other from non-payment for the work they have done. The building industry is by nature autocratically run and sometimes confrontational, so you will need a professional to act on your behalf and do any fighting for you.

Before the contract

Choosing a surveyor

Your initial task therefore is the appointment of a surveyor. Under no circumstances should a building contract be made the occasion for some trusted and worthy person in the block to demonstrate their managerial prowess in order to save the company money. It is a job for an experienced professional who will know how to deal with unforeseen problems as well as how to handle the contractor on your behalf.

When choosing a surveyor, a relatively small local firm is usually best, because you are more likely to get the continued attention of a senior person, possibly a partner. If you appoint a large firm you may be allocated a relatively junior and therefore less experienced surveyor. (He would, however, report to a senior partner on matters on which he needs advice.) The firm's fees may be higher, reflecting their prestige and expensive overheads. What you need is the more experienced man from the smaller local firm who will know the local contractors, will advise you better as to their comparative qualities, and, being new to your organisation, will want to make a good impression so as to establish a long-term relationship with the building. Even a relatively modest block is a substantial property and a smaller surveyor may well consider you an important and perhaps prestigious client. You will get what you pay for but fees at this level should be more negotiable. Try not to pay more than ten per cent of the contract sum in professional fees for the full surveyor's services. Some managing agents will have an in-house surveyors' department.

During a contract, a surveyor has considerable powers to amend and instruct further work according to his own professional standards. By appointing him to supervise a contract for you, you are accepting his authority to make these decisions. This emphasises the need to choose a surveyor with whom you can form a good working relationship.

Scaffolding contracts

A major external contract normally requires all or part of the building to be scaffolded. This will be the first time large areas of the property, usually uninspected for long periods, are made accessible. Regardless of the initial additional expenditure, some companies opt to have a scaffolding contract that is separate from that for redecorating and repairs, especially if the building has not been regularly maintained. The benefit is that if the scaffolding is erected before seeking tenders for the works, your surveyor will be able to draw up a full specification of the works to be done by inspecting roofs, chimney stacks, gable ends, gutters, drainpipes and windows in considerable detail. This close inspection produces an accurate description of the works to be carried out and leaves little scope for vagueness in a contractor's estimate when the job is put out to competitive tender.

Each contractor quoting for the works will also be able to inspect the building in detail and price his quote against an accurate specification. In particular, it will avoid the proliferation in the quotes of ***prime cost sums*** (which are for nominated and therefore known amounts. They usually refer to the cost of a specialist contractor or materials from a particular supplier which the surveyor has detailed in the specification; they should be exclusive of any profit to the main contractor and therefore not as variable as provisional sums) and ***provisional sums*** (which are estimates of work that cannot be accurately costed before the contract starts). There should be no surprising extra expenses. You will know not only that the whole of the area has been inspected closely by your surveyor, but also that the price accepted should be the full extent of your expenditure.

One disadvantage to leaving scaffolding in place for any length of time is that it creates a security risk by offering easy access to windows that, because of their elevated position, might not have been secured against break-ins. Security precautions include removing all ladders from ground level, lighting the scaffolding at night and having the scaffolding alarmed. There will always remain an element of risk, however, and residents should be advised in good time, and well before the scaffolding is erected, to take the necessary security precautions. They should fit locks to all windows and balcony doors.

However, since windows can only be satisfactorily repaired and painted when they are open, it is also essential that a system be put in operation during the contract to ensure coordination between the contractor and each resident. It is often practice for a landlord to issue the appropriate notice to tenants under the terms of the lease, informing them of his need to give the contractor access. Those who do not want to give access to their flats during the contract should, before the contract starts, be required to sign an appropriate instruction (see Appendix 4) accepting responsibility for the consequences.

For buildings with flat roofs, adjustable cradles are an alternative to scaffolding. They do not present such a risk to security since they can be lifted beyond reach when not in use. Although they may be cheaper to hire than scaffolding, they do not provide instant access to all parts of the building with the same ease as scaffolding.

The first contract

The first building contract under the new resident management company is always an important learning period for all involved. Apart from learning to work with a surveyor on a substantial project, it is a time to find out as much about the building as possible by following closely the activities of the appointed surveyor and where possible touring and inspecting with him. But in these circumstances he is the boss. Remember that you are doing the learning and have appointed him to advise. With the best will in the world, something is always likely to go wrong and a good surveyor will have his own way of dealing with problems. If he comes well recommended with a good track record, trust him.

It is always best to keep discussions about differences of opinion away from the workplace itself. When you ask the right questions you will usually find that you and he agree on most things. There are accepted and well-tried techniques of dealing with problems during a contract and a good surveyor will be applying them most of the time. It is important that his authority should never be challenged in front of a contractor, or indeed a difficult resident.

For the same reason, all residents should be told never to approach the contractor's workmen on site during a contract but to feed all queries through the surveyor or an agreed person, sometimes the contractor's supervisor on site. With your agreement the surveyor will, as part of his service, circulate information and questionnaires to tenants. In this way residents can be kept informed and feed back information, or ask questions about the contract. Tradesmen do not like to be watched by interfering tenants or to have their work commented upon by them. Meddling residents should be kept as far away from the contractor as possible.

Forms of contract

Your surveyor will use a well-established and widely used form of contract. These have been produced by the Royal Institution of Chartered Surveyors (RICS), the Royal Institute of British Architects (RIBA) and others sitting as the Joint Contracts Tribunal. These contracts are therefore known as JCT contracts and their website, *www.jctltd.co.uk*, contains the full range available. Your surveyor will choose which form of contract he will use depending upon the complexity of the specification and the duration of the works. The following are the most frequently used for block redecorations and refurbishments:

- The Intermediate IFC 98
- The Agreement for Minor Building Works 1998 Edition.

The second of the two is the one that all lessees who intend to carry out works in their own flats might use. Both forms of contract were created by the Joint Contracts Tribunal in 1998.

The chairman or appropriate director of the resident management company, being the employer, will normally be required to sign the contract. Although it is a complicated document, the best advice is: read it, note in some detail what you do not understand, and have a meeting with your surveyor at which all your queries can be answered. Your own knowledge of the building will be of considerable value and the surveyor may decide to amend either the contract or the specification on your recommendations. Your advice may prevent the site hut being placed in the least convenient position for residents, or cause access to and from site to be made more amenable. From here on, the surveyor takes control.

If the property is known to be in good repair and the supervising surveyor attends site regularly, it is quite normal to carry out a large redecorations contract without pre-scaffolding the building. This is done by using additional elevational drawings and a specification with a liberal allocation of provisional and prime cost sums.

The first contract of this kind that a lessee-owned company is involved with is seldom the least problematic and certainly never the cheapest. The way to get value for money is to get the best job you can afford, even if it is necessary to complete all the work in stages over two or three years. Experience has shown that, where a building has been in need of refurbishments, a thorough first contract has always paid dividends in the long run. The inconvenience passes quite quickly and no one gets the blame for insisting on cutting corners when a cheap job begins to deteriorate long before it is due to be repeated.

Stages in preparing and carrying out a contract

The preparation of the contract is the job of your surveyor. It is likely that he will also prepare some elevation drawings, depicting the building in some detail so that windows, balconies, rainwater pipes and other details can be identified clearly by the contractors who are quoting for the contract. These are especially useful if either the whole building is in some disrepair or parts of it are in varying stages of disrepair, needing specific identification and individual treatment.

The specification

A specification is a document prepared by the surveyor describing the work that is to be carried out (and is colloquially pronounced 'spess', not speck). It also defines what the contractual relationship between the company, as the employer, and the contractor will be. It is prepared for the benefit of the contractors, who will be asked to quote for the work so that each prices the works against identical information. A good specification will be written in clear English, with the headings and system of numbering clearly expressing your requirements as the employer.

It is usually divided into three parts.

1 Preliminaries and contract particulars

This describes the nature and location of the works, the type of contract, the names of the parties, specific additions or alterations to the standard form of contract, arrangements for working hours, supervision, insurance, and all matters relating to conduct on and use of the site.

2 Preambles or materials and workmanship

This establishes the class of workmanship required and the standards to be achieved. Materials can be identified by their British Standard (BS) number or catalogue reference, but quality of work can be more difficult to tie down and reference to other work is frequently used as a form of comparison. A more common way of dealing with this is to require work to be acceptable to the surveyor's own standards.

3 The works

This will form the bulk of the specification and will usually be divided into a number of schedules relating to different parts of the building. One large specification for a block which some years ago returned itself to its former, very handsome and distinctive condition, contained the following:

- Roof
- Windows and external joinery
- Elevations (the brickwork and stonework on the sides)
- Gable ends
- Balconies
- Decorations
- Rainwater plumbing (outside downpipes)
- Drains
- Completion (final tidying up).

Specifications are accessible documents. While their main use is in the obtaining of quotes and the carrying out and supervision of the contract itself, a copy to hand will help the management committee follow the process when the surveyor makes his progress reports.

Setting up and running the contract

The surveyor sends the draft contract documents, specification and relevant drawings to four or five recommended contractors. In doing this he initiates the process of 'competitive tendering'. He invites them to quote for the works by sending him their written tenders, based on the specification, by a certain date, usually one month ahead. He will probably have discussed with you your recommendations, and where agreed, these will be included.

No preference is given to any of the tendering contractors and each is allowed access to site for the purpose of estimating the cost of the works. Competitive tendering is a well-tried and tested way of ensuring fairness for those who tender and obtaining the best available quote for the employer.

Most contractors will use subcontractors for part of the works where their own tradesmen do not possess the appropriate skills. These will be smaller and more specialist firms such as roofers or electricians. Ideally, the contractor will have had a previous and successful working relationship with them. There may also be some 'nominated subcontractors' – specialists, such as stone repairers, known to the surveyor, who will be required by him to estimate as part of the overall contract and will eventually work for and under the chosen contractor with his subcontractors.

On the day when all tenders have to be submitted, and usually at a predetermined time and place, the surveyor opens all the tenders in the presence of an officer of the company and anyone else who has been invited. The names of the contractors are announced with the prices quoted. There can be a considerable disparity between the highest and lowest quote. From his own knowledge of quantities and the manner in which trades price for different jobs, the surveyor will have prepared his own figures of what the job was worth and will therefore spend some time examining all the quotes. Where appropriate, he will ask contractors to justify their figures, especially subtotals relating to particular parts of the contract. Contractors are usually keen to oblige, because such queries suggest that their quote is being given serious consideration.

After a close examination of the figures, the surveyor recommends a quote. This may not be the lowest, for any number of reasons. For example, he may feel either that he has not received adequate answers to his questions, or that the job cannot be done to the required standard within the figure quoted. His recommendation will then be put to the company for its decision.

It is the responsibility of the company to make the final choice of contractor, but the surveyor's advice will bear heavily on this decision. The contract will be offered to the successful firm and, if accepted, the contract is signed and work commences in accordance with a site programme. This is a plan showing the course of the contract, what work will be done in each week and which trades will be on site. This will all be scheduled to end on the contracted completion date.

How the works are supervised

The contractor will allocate his own foreman to supervise his tradesmen and the subcontractors. It will be his job to liaise with your surveyor who, on a substantial contract, will normally attend site at least once each week. These visits will take the form of formal site meetings with inspections of the previous week's work.

If a variation to the specified work is necessary, this can only be authorised by the surveyor (issuing a surveyor's instruction) on behalf of the company. Surveyor's instructions are usually issued as a result of discussions that have taken place at the site meetings. The surveyor and the contractor (and, where appropriate, a subcontractor) inspect together. Standards of work are checked and instructions are issued to repeat any work that is considered unacceptable.

At the end of the working period and before a certificate of practical completion is issued, the surveyor makes a careful inspection of the whole job in order to draw up the *'snagging list'*. This is a detailed list of all items that require attention and is given to the contractor, who will be expected to carry out the necessary work before any more money is handed over.

It is worth noting that when residents are made aware of this important part of the procedure, there is less anxiety that unfinished matters may have been overlooked during the contract. Very often defects are intentionally left to the end so that they can be 'picked up' on the final snagging list.

Payment

The contractor is paid in stages throughout the duration of the contract. At prearranged intervals, an inspection by the surveyor will be followed by a valuation of the work carried out to date. The surveyor will prepare an 'interim certificate' which will be issued to the company for payment. By contract, the company will have fourteen days in which to pay the contractor.

The contract also protects the company and will allow the surveyor to make a deduction, usually five per cent, part of which is held for a period after the works are finished. This period is known as the *'defects liability period'*. It may last for as much as six months to a year after the works finish, during which time the contractor is required to make good any defects relating to the work.

When the works have effectively been completed – hopefully on the agreed completion date – *'practical completion'* takes place. After the surveyor is satisfied that the snagging list has been properly dealt with, he issues a *'certificate of practical completion'*.

Under certain circumstances, the contract is allowed to overrun. The contractor must give good reasons for requesting this, and sometimes detailed reports from the Meteorological Office appear appended to the minutes of site meetings when the weather has been particularly inclement.

The other reason contracts overrun is that the surveyor has instructed the contractor to carry out additional works and has consequently granted an extension.

If the works overrun without the agreement of the surveyor, the contract will require the contractor to forfeit agreed sums for each week the contract is late finishing. These are called *'liquidated damages'*; contractually they should fairly reflect the loss to the company for the delay and not unduly penalise the contractor.

Practical completion is a watershed rather than the end of matters, because it is then that the following take effect.

- The final valuation begins which the company must settle in the same way as other valuations.

- The 'defects liability period' begins during which the contractor must make good any defective work. This used to be a six-month period but now can be as long as a year.

- Half of the five per cent retention sum held by the company must be released to the contractor.

- The contractor ceases to be liable for liquidated damages.

- The contractor is no longer responsible for insuring the site.

After practical completion, the contractor provides the surveyor with his accounts and documentation relating to the works. Within twenty-eight days of receiving the paperwork, the surveyor, subject to any outstanding faults having been remedied by the contractor, issues the *'final certificate'*. This is a complete financial analysis of the works from beginning to end and includes all monies so far paid as well as those owing. This the company must pay within the stipulated time period.

Finally, after the defects liability period expires, the contractor is required to make good all outstanding defects to his work. Last of all, the company releases the two and a half per cent of the total contract value that it has been holding during this final period.

ACTION

Your surveyor will have a more intimate understanding of the contract as it affects you, and at the end of your first contract you should be in a position to make an assessment both of your understanding of the process and your relationship with your surveyor. Discuss the problems you have both encountered during the contract and think about how these can be dealt with next time.

After the works are completed, reread the contract and specification and relate their content to what has happened.

READING

LEASE, *Appointment of a Surveyor/Management Audits* – free booklet.

CHAPTER 12

Managing the future

This chapter brings together the substance of the whole book and treats each aspect as a matter for continuing attention. It is therefore both a summary and a point of departure.

It shows how the different managerial components of the business are made routine. It does not try to create a fixed pattern of decision-making but rather attempts to show how individual companies can go about this for themselves. It introduces some new information in the areas of security and Health and Safety, but in the main concentrates on uncomplicated ways of devising an annual round of decision-making.

It is easy to lose sight of the peculiarities of the lessee-owned company that distinguish it from other businesses – and indeed from the business of which the property was part before being bought or managed by the lessees. The building is no longer a business resource to be used by the landlord for the purpose of maximising profits. You may aim to make a surplus on operations in any given year in order to add to the reserve fund, but you will not be making a profit. The Memorandums and Articles of Association of lessee-owned companies do not usually include the ultimate aim of selling the property.

Companies that make profits have a clear view of the relationship between quality and quantity. A commercial business uses quality to improve quantity. In other words, it will try to produce a better-quality item, so that it does better in the marketplace, in order that more of its items are sold, with the aim of outselling the competition. In a lessee-owned company, quantity serves quality. In other words, amounts of money, time and effort are applied in order to establish and maintain the standards of the property, services and amenities at a level where the lessee/shareholders feel they are getting value for money.

Of course this criterion suffers badly from subjective judgement and individual opinion. What pleases one resident falls short of the expectations of a second, and may be considered extravagant by a third. A survey of service charges in your area and a review of standards, services and amenities enjoyed by other residents, provides a useful injection of objectivity and a measure against which you can assess how well you are really doing.

Implementing decisions

A great deal has already been said in Chapter 4 about meetings. But how do you keep them effective as the months and years go by? As the company settles down, and after the first wave of enthusiasm has subsided, it is advisable to set up a programme of regular meetings throughout the year, each of which addresses a specific matter – for example staff, contracts, accounts and service charges. Assuming that the financial year end was 31st December, a typical programme of management committee meetings might run as follows:

Meeting 1	March – Accounts, service charges etc
	May – AGM
Meeting 2	June – Staffing and Health and Safety
Meeting 3	September – Maintenance and service contracts
Meeting 4	December – Residents' matters and amenities.

The underlying idea of such a programme is that the main subject matter of meetings is used to order the content of successive meetings. If you have instructed a managing agent, this type of routine is of considerable benefit. Much of the preparation will be carried out by the managing agent and there are likely to be few other meetings outside those programmed. As the years go by, one would hope to settle down to a good working relationship, in which the managing agent is trusted to get on with the business of administering the task on behalf of the company and knows when he is to report and what the main subject matter will be.

Those who have chosen to manage their own block need to apply a degree of self-discipline regarding the frequency of meetings. A set programme of meetings is useful. At first, management committee meetings will occur at about monthly intervals. As soon as appropriate, say after one year, bimonthly meetings should be possible, although many like to retain more frequent meetings.

The ideal is a programme of regular quarterly meetings, with others called as necessary. This is possible if members have been allocated roles and are active in sub-committees or working parties producing simple reports. In this way, active lessees find they sustain their interest in the formal business of managing the block.

Most matters allocated to a sub-committee or a working party for their attention can be dealt with in a short report on one side of a sheet of paper, stating:

- Its terms of reference
- Its recommendations
- Supporting evidence
- Other matters taken into consideration
- Authors of the report and date.

A more comprehensive discussion can take place in the full meeting and the decision will be minuted in the appropriate way.

Inevitably the membership of the board and management committee will change as time goes by. Establish a simple format for introducing new committee members to the business of the meeting, even if it is simply to provide a copy of the code of working practice (see Chapter 4) and pass on the previous member's file. There is a legal requirement to inform Companies House, on the appropriate form, when a director is either appointed or resigns.

Much smaller blocks will probably want to avoid all this after the first year or so, and opt for the alternative of abandoning formal meetings and, instead, circulating accounts. In either case it is of paramount importance to keep shareholders informed, and, if nothing of any moment has happened for some time, to assure them that this is normal.

Above all, avoid meetings for their own sake and the attendant emergence of block politics. If there is any sign that this is beginning to happen, get the matter discussed by the board and draw special attention to directors' duties, the accepted codes of conduct in operation and the Memorandum and Articles of Association of the company.

Managing the service charge and accounts

The management of the block's money is of such central importance to the whole business that it must have pride of place in the annual round of meetings. It is normal to decide on the following year's estimated service charge at around the time that audited accounts are received and considered by the directors – say one month before the AGM. The schedule suggested above assumes that the AGM will be in May and that the finances will therefore be considered at a meeting around March. The director responsible for finance, the accountant or the managing agent will be required to present the appropriate information to this regularly scheduled yearly meeting.

This meeting is the time to consider all matters relating to the finances of the block. It will:

- Review the past year's expenditure.
- Estimate next year's expenditure.
- Set the service charge for the following year.
- If the company has a bank account in its own name, check the bank mandate to make sure it is up to date. (It is more likely that the bank account is administered by the managing agent since it is becoming increasingly difficult for individual lessee-owned companies to do so themselves. New government restrictions introduced to prevent money laundering make it almost impossible for a resident management company to administer its own bank account where there may be a turnover of directors and consequently a need periodically to change the company's bank mandate.)
- Review instructions to the bank.
- Inspect the bank statements to see that the balance corresponds with the company's records and the terms under which the bank holds your account.

All this will be carried out in preparation for the AGM.

Managing staff

Part of the responsibilities of a managing agent is to recruit, supervise and communicate with staff in the building. The quarterly meeting that considers staff will require his attendance and it will be on the basis of his contributions and advice to the meeting that the board will normally make their decisions. However, those who have chosen not to appoint a managing agent will need to give very careful consideration to their responsibilities here. For those who are new to the responsibilities of an employer, there is an excellent handbook for small firms called *Employing People* – published by ACAS *(www.acas.org.uk)*.

Expenditure on staff will differ from block to block, depending on the number and type of staff. Some blocks will have uniformed resident porters and their auxiliary staff, while others may be adequately served by a part-time caretaker/cleaner/handyman. There is seldom any reason to introduce complicated personnel procedures to cover such matters as pay, appraisal and training but the landlord does have obligations in law

Managing the future

which should be understood and observed; the 'staff' meeting is a good time to review them.

The following sections address the main areas concerning staff.

Pay

The main purpose of reviewing staff annually is to set their pay for the forthcoming year and to assess their performance over the previous year. In the meeting schedule above, this item has been programmed for a June meeting since most pay rises come into effect around mid-year, but there is no hard and fast rule.

There are different schools of thought about pay. The two most common can be described as follows. The first says: pay your staff as well as you can afford to and motivate them through their job, allowing them to accept responsibility for what they do over as wide a range of activities as possible. The second says that people will not do anything unless you make them and therefore money should be used as an incentive to get the best out of them.

This is not the place for a full discussion of these opposing views; suffice it to say that different people respond to different methods of pay for many reasons. But if you find the right person who responds to the first approach, you are likely to have a good pay policy.

Performance

Caretakers, porters and cleaners spend a great deal of time alone at work and have to be trusted to get on with their duties. Apart from an annual Christmas bonus to imply general satisfaction, there are no effective ways of fixing a bonus to their performance.

Never give a bonus for attendance. Attending work is part of the contract. Staff should not be paid twice for the same thing.

A bonus soon becomes expected and resented if it is not thought to be big enough. Tell your staff what your policy is and if they are paid well they will want to work well and stay. Inspect regularly and let staff know whether you are happy or not. Those that constantly fall below standard should be warned in the proper way and, if standards do not improve, replaced by staff who can justify the pay. If there are few complaints about staff during the course of a year, if the caretaker is seen about and the common parts are kept clean, then this is as good an indicator as any that staff performance is adequate.

Contracts of employment

The directors should remind themselves of the contents of the contracts of employment to which the company is party. These should be checked to ensure that they are lawful and up to date and do not restrict staff in carrying out their proper duties. However, any alteration to them, unless it is a new legal requirement, usually requires the consent of the staff concerned. Check also that new staff have a copy of their contract.

Duties

The written staff duties should be reviewed at this meeting to see if they need updating. This is an area where staff should be allowed their own input, and can be the subject of a separate discussion with staff before the meeting. While duties should not be reduced, circumstances often determine that they should be changed. Furthermore, it is another way of showing staff that their opinions and contributions are valued.

Materials and equipment

This is an area frequently overlooked or not given the importance it requires when the periodic review of staff matters is being carried out. Substandard materials and equipment limit performance. Some staff become attached to old, outdated and ineffective equipment such as vacuum cleaners, or proudly boast that they have mended a set of ladders so many times. Not only is it a waste of time to mend them, but equipment can become unreliable and sometimes dangerous. There is a Health and Safety duty in law on both employer and employee where materials and equipment are concerned (see below).

Both cleaning materials and equipment should be inspected with staff, as well as tools used in day-to-day maintenance, to ensure that they remain effective and appropriate and that standards are not being allowed to fall through the pursuit of ultimately false economies. The meeting can then discuss these matters to decide if a provision should be put in the following year's estimates for new equipment.

Communications with staff

Despite living and working in residential buildings, porters and caretakers can live very lonely lives. This may be by choice, but there are a number of obvious consequences. Work habits frequently determine that in spending so much time alone, they have no other advice to take than that which they give themselves. As a result, habits sometimes replace duties and these then become the job. Responsible staff must be kept in touch with the company. The 'staff director' should be able to report that fortnightly or monthly meetings have taken place throughout the year, sometimes amounting to no more than an informed chat, that certain instructions were given, advice taken and that the results were positive. The very essence of good communication of this type is that it should be informed, frequent and two-way.

Managing Health and Safety

The company's responsibility for Health and Safety in law is comprehensive and onerous. Unless you are a small building with available in-house expertise, then the services of a Health and Safety professional are, in the first instance, the most sensible way forward. This section attempts to identify the scope of this responsibility and suggest ways of getting the best information and advice.

The company is responsible in law for the health and safety of its employees, contractors working on site as well visitors to the building. Health and Safety at Work law is covered by both statute law and common law. They both cover similar areas and whereas the statute law is precise and detailed and carries legal penalties, the safety requirements of common law have a much wider scope and might best be expressed as the employer's 'duty of care'. It is possible for an employer to be liable for damages in common law for a civil offence and yet not be in breach of statute law. A comparison can be made between the two.

Common law requires the employer to exercise a duty of care towards his employees, contractors and visitors by providing:

- A safe working place as well as a safe access to it (eg common parts, lifts, boiler)
- Safe working equipment – tools, ladders, materials etc
- A safe system of work – methods and procedures
- Proper job instruction – training
- Competent employees – who are not a danger to others.

Non-compliance is a civil offence. Thus an injured person can take action against the employer for personal compensation.

The Health and Safety at Work Act 1974 is the relevant statute law. Together with subsequent regulations, it places, as far as is reasonably practical, the following general duties on employers to:

- Ensure the health and safety of employees
- Provide a safe plant and system of work
- Ensure the safe use, handling, storage and transport of articles and substances
- Provide information, instruction, training and supervision to employees
- Maintain a safe place of work and access to it.

Non-compliance is a criminal offence. Legal action may be an Improvement or Prohibition Notice which would be issued by an Inspector of the Health and Safety Executive. At worst, prosecution can be the result.

Where there are more than five employees then there must be a written Health and Safety policy stating who is responsible for Health and Safety and what aspects of Health and Safety it covers.

This is a responsibility that would be delegated to a managing agent. Since the act of delegation does not release the board from the responsibility, it would make sense to ensure that the caretaker and/or a designated director attend a Health and Safety course suitable for residential properties. As knowledge and expertise are developed they will be in a position to report to the board on their annual risk assessment inspections. There are many consultancies that run courses. Advice on an appropriate Health and Safety training courses can be got from the Health and Safety Executive (see below).

Some particular responsibilities are worth emphasising. It is the responsibility of the company to carry out a complete *risk assessment* of the building on an annual basis. This may be the point at which you decide to seek the advice of a Health and Safety professional. New employees must, in law, be told of the company's own rules on safety and any special hazards must be drawn to their attention. It is a requirement that employees must be reminded regularly of their responsibility to ensure that the workplace and the methods of work used are safe. These can be done initially through Health and Safety training.

The annual directors' June 'Staffing and Health and Safety' meeting is an appropriate time to record formally that a meeting has been held with staff to remind them of their responsibilities and that the risk assessment inspection has been carried out.

Managing the future

Information on Health and Safety

There are a number of useful sources of information on Health and Safety. You may download free Health and Safety leaflets from the official Health and Safety Executive (HSE) website, *www.hse.gov.uk*. Otherwise they can be obtained by telephoning their special free pamphlet number (08702 249 090). In particular, their guidance booklets on the implementation of safety policies, and their construction sheets on chemical cleaners, solvents, personal protective equipment and the control of substances hazardous to health (COSHH) are useful. Your Health and Safety adviser should supply you with a comprehensive 'Health and Safety Inspection Checklist' that fits the particular requirements and character of your building and which will be the basis of your risk assessment inspection routine.

The following are well-known charitable organisations with specific expertise in the field, who can provide useful information and training.

- RoSPA (Royal Society for the Prevention of Accidents) provide safety training, consultancy in occupational safety and produce a range of safety posters. Their website is *www.rospa.com*
- The Red Cross and St John's Ambulance both run First Aid courses from basic to advanced levels and some specifically cover Occupational First Aid. Their respective websites and phone numbers are *www.redcross.org.uk* (020 7235 5454) and *www.sja.org.uk* (08700 10 49 50).

Fire hazards and precautions

The annual risk assessment inspection also covers fire hazards and precautions. Therefore, the June annual meeting should also review fire hazards, access, alarms and extinguishers.

The common parts of the building are frequently designated as areas of escape from flats in the event of fire. Items left in the common parts will usually be deemed to constitute a fire hazard because they restrict escape and access for the fire brigade.

Where access to a flat roof constitutes an escape route, the doors should be inspected regularly, as well as any device facilitating escape, such as a break-glass key box. All common parts should be kept clear of inflammable materials, not forgetting the roof space area. Residents have been known to use the roof space for storing inflammable items such as papers, books and unwanted soft furnishings. Rubbish also collects at the bottom of lift shafts; the shaft itself, with a skylight above it, often provides a natural flue.

The law does not require the installation of a common fire alarm in residential blocks of flats. A common fire alarm is usually only appropriate where the evacuation of the building can be controlled. This is usually neither practicable nor necessary where many flats are remote from the site of an emergency. In modern buildings and some older ones, such as those with a filler joist construction, each flat may be fire resistant for a safe period of time and should be secure until the fire brigade attends. Unnecessary evacuation can create a certain amount of danger to occupants if they enter smoke-filled common parts and open doors can create added draught for the fire.

Fires that start from within flats cause the most deaths by fire in residential blocks. The most effective and inexpensive way of dealing with this risk is the installation of a smoke alarm. The recommended way of smothering a kitchen pan fire is with a standard fire blanket. Individual residents can be encouraged to obtain them from a DIY or Health and Safety source.

A useful and frequently recommended publication is *Fire Safety: An Employer's Guide* by the Home Office and the Health and Safety Executive, available from the Stationery Office *(www.tso.co.uk)*. Further guidance on fire safety in the home is also published by the government (tel: 0207 273 2756).

Your insurers for the block need to be informed of some or all of these matters which may affect your premium. However, while it is better to be safe than sorry, beware the keen salesman, for example of insurance or fire extinguishers, who is skilled in creating an anxiety in a potential client. Choose your adviser carefully and act on their advice.

Notifying residents

Residents need to be kept informed about the company's fire precaution policy. General advice should include information on fire prevention in the home. The following is a list of possible contents.

- What to do in case of fire (eg depending upon the building – call the fire brigade, close all non-access doors and windows and leave taking everyone with you).

- Fire exits and escape routes (draw everybody's attention to the need to keep all common parts clear of hazards of every type).

- Use of extinguishers (explain the proper uses of the different types of extinguisher).

- Fire alarms (eg regular testing of domestic smoke alarms).

The common parts of the property, staircases and hallways, will usually contain fire extinguishers with adjacent notices containing instructions on their use. The entrance area is often a good place to site a notice containing 'In Case of Fire' information. The full policy, as provided by your adviser, could be part of the tenant's pack.

Managing maintenance and service contracts

Maintenance contracts should also be reviewed on an annual basis, both to ensure that the contracted company is performing to the requirements of the contract, and, where contracts are for one year or coming to an end, to review the market. The suggested schedule programmes this meeting for September, which is a time when the building should be checked over to prepare it for the winter, although contracts may for historical reasons have different renewal dates. In a large block, either the managing agent or sub-committee on contracts would keep contracts under review all year and would report their advice to this meeting.

The following five sections address the main areas concerning managing maintenance and service contracts.

Pest control

The subject of pests is, understandably, a sensitive one. People do not like admitting that they have an infestation of cockroaches, ants or fleas. Few residential blocks are entirely free of pests of one sort or another. Some buildings have a very serious infestation which residents have been too embarrassed to discuss. One should always be prepared to tackle the issue head on: inform all residents that the company intends to deal with it and ask for complete cooperation. The lease will require this, anyway. Very often pest control contracts are underused. Experience has shown that treating flats individually is a waste of time and that a coordinated approach is necessary.

There are a number of specialists in this field. Since the companies are in competition with one another, it does no harm to compare their prices regularly. A contract of this nature may entail regular visits to the premises, or simply require the specialist company to respond to requests to attend to deal with problems on an ad hoc basis. The contract may include all forms of pest eradication such as cockroaches, ants, woodworm, fleas, rats and mice – even swarms of bees, not to mention pigeons. Pest control not only attempts to deal with a major problem; it also helps to keep the problem at bay. Make sure you are getting your regular visits by requiring the caretaker to ask the operative to sign his diary on each visit.

Insurance

Each year, before the appropriate meeting, write to or phone your insurance broker to obtain answers to any queries you may have about your policies. You may have a building policy, an engineering policy to cover a boiler, and a policy to cover passenger lifts. You should also have a Directors and Officers Insurance Policy. What you ask your broker will depend on what you need to know in any given year. This might include forecasts of any changes in premium over the following twelve months, requests to obtain quotes to extend cover, for example during a refurbishment contract, or indeed to look at the market to improve the insurance you already have. This last is usually only requested when an agreement of more than one year is coming to an end. The information you get should be sufficient for the committee to make its annual decision.

Leaseholders need to know what they are responsible for insuring and what the block insurance covers. This information should be part of the Welcome Pack (see Appendix 3). The company insures the building and fixtures. The lessee should insure the contents of his flat which is best defined as being the carpets, curtains and furniture and any other article which would be removed if he sold his flat. In addition, the lessees' policy should cover accidental damage to other flats.

Boiler (central heating and hot water)

A boiler usually has a service contract requiring the contracted maintenance company to service the boiler regularly. It is helpful if the engineer sends you a completed pro forma confirming that the service was carried out, what it entailed and notifying you of the present condition of the boiler.

Again, there are a number of boiler maintenance companies. While contracts are often for a number of years, it is good practice to seek information from other companies occasionally to compare contracts and costs.

Lift

If you have a passenger lift, two companies should be visiting on a regular basis, the insurance company and the service engineers. The company insuring the lift will visit regularly to inspect and will usually send you a copy of their observations. These details should keep you informed about the condition of the lift and will tell you if work is required. These observations should not be confused with a service report. The company that carries out the servicing of the lifts operates independently of the insurance company and should be regularly checked to ensure that they attend to the lifts and that any faults observed and reported by the insurance company are dealt with immediately.

If your company is operating without a managing agent, it should be the responsibility of a nominated director or committee member to inform themselves about the safety regulations governing passenger lifts. Under these circumstances, the service engineer should be required to sign the caretaker's diary, or leave a card, to confirm that he has attended site.

Planned maintenance

Property maintenance contracts should state what is to be maintained, when and how. On a large building, much of the work of planned maintenance is taken up with inspection and testing to make sure that a specific service is functioning or a particular element of the building is sound. It lends itself to checklists and simple reports; in fact, these should be insisted upon and each maintenance visit should be recorded in the caretaker's diary. This is the basis of the information used by the director responsible for maintenance in his annual report.

The standard of maintenance can always be assessed by the number of complaints received from residents. Obviously, complaints can be misleading, so if there is any suggestion that you are not getting value for money, and your attempt to sort out a matter with the contractor falls on deaf ears, ask your surveyor to carry out the same inspection programme directly after one has been made. There are enough good firms in the business to ensure that you can get good service. But as with many things, familiarity with a building not only increases knowledge of it but also encourages corner-cutting, and it is no bad thing to change your contractor occasionally. If you do so, do it as amicably as possible. Contractors are less upset at losing a contract if they feel they have a chance of getting it back later.

Managing residents' matters and amenities

This is the fourth of the annual round of meetings and in this schedule is programmed to be held in December. If one meeting each year is allocated to the function of discussing difficult matters relating to residents, the very fact that it is a routine ensures that there is an appropriate time to address these matters. It also avoids allegations that the meeting has been called to discuss a particular resident and concentrates minds to make decisions at the appointed meeting. Difficult decisions are too often the subject of procrastination.

The following three sections address the main areas concerning managing residents' matters and amenities.

Irregularities of occupancy

The items on this agenda would refer to continuous complaints about particular residents, uninhabited flats, unauthorised subletting and unnotified alterations to internal arrangements. The company may decide not to get involved with inter-flat disputes if the covenants are not mutually enforceable. Empty flats that create a risk of any kind, irregular occupation, or where alterations to the structure have been made without authorisation, are all examples that may require further investigation. Evidence should be put to the meeting so that clear and speedy decisions about each can be arrived at.

Security

A directors' meeting with security on its agenda is most likely to be reviewing access to restricted areas, locks, keys and their authorised users. There will usually be a number of doors in common use as well as cupboards containing electricity boxes and other equipment. Each of these will probably have a lock and key. The company, as landlord, usually authorises a group of people to hold master keys and have access to the key safe, if there is one. This will almost certainly include the caretaker or most senior member of staff. Before the directors' meeting, all keys will be inspected and the appropriate locks tested.

Unless the lease clearly states that the landlord is responsible for security, the company should make it clear to all residents where the landlord's responsibility lies. If the company accepts responsibility for the total security of the common parts, and flats are broken into, the landlord may be held responsible for permitting access to the stairways and therefore to flats. Avoid the security salesman whose attempts to make you feel insecure are part of his job of selling security. The local police crime prevention officer will tell you about the latest technology for nothing. Above all, be guided by your responsibilities under the lease.

No matter how technically efficient, communal door entry systems are inadequate security devices and only have a marginal deterrent effect

Managing the future

because residents are so ready to let people they do not know into the building. Some blocks insist that the security of each individual flat starts and ends at the front door of each individual flat. It is then the responsibility of each lessee to provide adequate locks and other security devices for their own protection. In this respect intruder alarms are usually discouraged, because their propensity for causing unnecessary disturbance and annoyance is usually thought to far outweigh their supposed protection.

The most common (and usually adequate) forms of security for a flat are the installation in a front door of two security locks, one of them a deadlock, with coded and numbered keys, set about eighteen inches apart, hinge bolts, a security chain to hold the door ajar when open, and a magnifying spy-hole in the centre of the door so that visitors can be recognised. Where leaseholders of ground-floor flats feel particularly vulnerable, sliding security grilles fitted to the inside of windows are a very effective means of protection.

Amenities

Garages, parking spaces and storage lockers pose few problems apart from the administration of their use. These problems, which are usually associated with either allocation or abuse, again, have to be handled quickly and effectively to avoid recurrent distractions from the proper business of the company (see Chapter 3 – amenities director). The four matters that need to be reviewed annually are:

- Income and expenditure
- Repairs and maintenance
- The current use to which the amenities are put
- A review of the waiting list.

The meeting can decide if and when the company needs to carry out repairs which are usually financed by rental income. The agreements allowing the use of amenities can be reviewed and assessed in each case to see whether the user is keeping the agreement. Amenity contracts of a set duration may need to be renewed or notification given of termination. A great many problems are solved by checking the state of the waiting list to make sure that everyone on it is still eligible to rent and use the amenity they require.

Conclusion

As you become more familiar with the management of your block and begin to settle into the type of routine that this chapter is advocating, then the whole business will become much easier. The most difficult part is setting it up and getting to know other lessees in a formal business setting. Although the advice in this book is based upon an extensive knowledge of managing residential properties, it is impossible here to predict every possible circumstance. The very substantial 'people' content involved in the management of blocks of flats ensures that there will always be that element of surprise which never ceases to fascinate, regardless of who is involved and what their intentions might be.

READING

Advisory, Conciliation and Arbitration Service (2003) *Employing People: Handbook for Small Firms*.

The Health and Safety Executive (1993) *Writing Your Health and Safety Policy Statement,* HSE Books, ISBN 0717604241.

APPENDIX 1

The Annual General Meeting

Preparation

The Notice of the Annual General Meeting should be sent out by the company secretary to all shareholders at least 21 clear days prior to the meeting. The Notice should contain:

- A statement that the meeting is an Annual General Meeting
- Details of the date, place and time of the meeting
- The agenda, including the wording of all resolutions
- Details of the rights of members to appoint proxies to vote for them
- Notice of the final day by which items for any other business should be received by the company secretary for inclusion as formal business.

The company secretary should also send out, with the agenda, copies of the annual accounts and directors' report. If the meeting is going to be a larger one, do not forget to book the venue in good time.

Typical agenda

The agenda is the order of business. Some items require the meeting to vote on a resolution such as the appointment of directors and auditors. Other items are simply 'received' by the meeting such as the accounts and Annual Report of Directors.

1. Notice convening the meeting
2. Minutes of the previous AGM
3. Audited accounts and Report of Directors – to be received and considered by the meeting
4. Appointment of auditors
5. Election of directors
6. Any other business.

(It is becoming increasingly common for shareholders to be asked to approve the next year's budget at the AGM and less common, for practical reasons and timescales, for the minutes of the previous AGM to be considered or approved.)

ACTION

The company secretary must send the following documents to Companies House:

- **Annual Return** (Form 363s). The 's' is for 'shuttle'. Companies House will send you the form containing the details they have on your company, which you should confirm or amend and return to them with a list of current shareholders accompanied by the filing fee.

- **Change of directors or secretary or change of particulars** (Form 288a & b). This form you should obtain yourself from Companies House and send it in if changes have been made.

- **Audited accounts.** Your company will have an Accounting Reference Date which will be your financial end of year and the date to which the accounts are made up. You are required to send a copy of your audited accounts to Companies House within ten months of your Accounting Reference Date.

The company secretary should also write up the **minutes of the meeting** for vetting by the Chairman and circulation to all shareholders.

Keep **photocopies** of all items to be put into the statutory books.

APPENDIX 2A

Building works and the refurbishment of flats

The following conditions have been compiled for leaseholders applying for permission to carry out building works, alterations and improvements to their flats. The Conditions for Contractors apply to all categories of works.

The following items require permission from the freeholder

1   Installation of new central heating.
2   The fitting of a new kitchen system.
3   The fitting of a new bathroom, the rearrangement of bathroom and sanitary fittings, or new extra installations, eg WCs, baths, shower units, wash hand basins or bidets.
4   Installing new windows or entrance doors (in some instances planning permission may be required).
5   Structural alterations affecting the walls of a flat, including the removal of old walls or the building of new walls, the formation of new openings and doorways etc.

Conditions for all categories of works

1   The works must comply with all statutory requirements, Acts of Parliament, Building Regulations and the terms of the lease.
2   A full list of works must be submitted.
3   The name, address and telephone number of the contractor must be supplied, and a copy of the contractor's All Risk and Liability insurance policy.
4   A deposit must be lodged with the managing agents according to the scale of work.

The deposit is returnable on completion less fees payable to the managing agents. The fees of the company structural engineer may also be deducted. Where it is necessary for a structural engineer to be employed to provide calculations, we would suggest that such appointment should be mutually agreed to prevent the need for calculations to be checked by the company separately.

Any costs involving extra cleaning or repair of damage to common parts, the removal of discarded appliances or rubbish, or any other costs arising from the resident's failure to ensure that his contractors adhere to the Conditions for Contractors will also be deducted.

The authorisation and approval of these works does not form part of the managing agents' fee structure, and basic charges will vary from a minimum of £50 dependent on the work involved in items 1–4 and a minimum fee of £250 for item 5 according to works involved. Residents who carefully follow these instructions will be charged the minimum providing their contractors comply with the Conditions for Contractors.

The balance of the deposit will be returned for items 1, 2 and 3 when the resident's plumber provides a certificate stating that the new plumbing system and appliances have been tested and left in good working order. Where new toilets are concerned, approval of the Building Control Officer is also required. Deposits for work detailed in item 4 will be returned when the company surveyor has approved the completed installation.

Deposits against structural work (item 5) are returned on receipt of a letter from the structural engineer, confirming that he has inspected the work while in progress and is satisfied that his specification has been followed correctly.

The managing agents reserve the right to deduct from the deposit sums of money up to £50 a day for infringement by the builders of the Conditions for Contractors. The penalties will be credited to the Service Charge Fund of the appropriate block. The payment of the deposit will be taken as confirmation of the leaseholder's agreement to these conditions.

5   No permission will be granted to leaseholders who are in arrears of service charge.

6   Where appropriate, a copy of the Building Notice must be submitted to the managing agents.

7 No work must commence before permission has been confirmed. Documents and deposits should be submitted four weeks before the required start date.

Additional requirements where new central heating is to be installed

The residents must obtain approval for the siting of the flues. Balanced flues must only be sited on the rear of the building, and fitted with the correct external cover. Where a conventional flue is used, the chimney must be lined with a Kopex-type lining. Top- and third-floor flats are not always suitable for combi-boilers owing to insufficient water pressure. Appropriate instruments must be used to check pressure for suitability. The deposit required for this category of work is £300.

Additional requirements where a new kitchen is to be fitted

All new waste pipes must be fitted in accordance with good practice and correctly sealed into the wall with cement. All external pipework must be installed in maintenance-free black plastic – not grey plastic painted black (except where there is a requirement for cast iron). Any consequential damage to external pipework must be repaired. It is a statutory requirement that waste disposal must be plumbed into the adjacent soil pipe. Under no circumstances must the waste from these appliances be fed into a hopper or the existing sink or bathroom waste. The deposit required for this category of work is £300.

Additional requirements where bathroom appliances or WCs are installed, in a new position, or where additional appliances are installed

Applications must be accompanied by detailed plans showing the new position of the appliances, the route of the waste pipe and the drop. The point at which the waste joins the existing system must also be shown together with a detailed plan of the run of any waste or soil stack and detailed plans of any new manhole. The plans must be sent to be approved by the Building Control Officer. Confirmation that it has been approved must be submitted with your application. A plastic waterproof membrane must be installed under the bathroom floor covering if ceramic or lino tiles are laid. Where possible, showers should be tanked and fitted with an external overflow. All external pipework must be installed in maintenance-free black plastic – not grey plastic painted black. All new waste pipes must be fitted externally with ninety-degree elbows directed neatly into the waste hopper and correctly sealed into the wall with cement. Any consequential damage to external brickwork must be repaired. Old pipework should be replaced in copper. Isolator valves should be fitted to appliances and stopcocks to isolate the flat circuit from the mains or down services from the tanks in the loft. The deposit for this category of work is £300.

Additional conditions applying to structural alterations

1   Applications for structural alterations must be accompanied by detailed plans showing the layout of the flat before and after, with the walls to be removed and the new walls to be built highlighted in colour.

2   If the walls are non-load-bearing stud, written confirmation of this from a qualified surveyor or architect or structural engineer will be sufficient. The deposit required for this category of work will vary from £500 to £1,500 according to the scale of the work.

3   If the walls are load-bearing, the application must be accompanied by load calculations from a qualified structural engineer who is covered by Professional Indemnity insurance with a correctly prepared plan and a specification showing the proposal for the alternative bearing of the load. This must give full details of the size and support arrangement for lintels, RSJs and box frames. Written approval from the Building Control Officer should accompany the application and a Building Notice be filed before the work commences. The deposit required for this category of work is £750 for minor works to load-bearing walls, and £1,500 for major load-bearing walls supporting the main structure of the building.

4   If scaffolding is to be used, the type and position are to be agreed with the managing agents before erection. Details for the duration of the scaffolding must also be agreed in advance.

5   The appointment of a qualified surveyor to commission, oversee and approve the works is recommended.

If any unauthorised building work is undertaken, we will have served a Notice under Section 146 of the Law of Property Act 1925,

the cost of which will be borne by the lessee. Any bank or building society with registered mortgage interest in a flat will be notified of the breach in the terms of the lease so that they can protect their security.

APPENDIX 2B

Standard Conditions for Contractors

1. These conditions apply to all contractors carrying out work on behalf of leaseholders and involving work inside and outside their flats.

2. Lessees must notify the managing agents and obtain the permission of the freeholder before any works involving plumbing, windows and entrance doors, or structural alterations take place. There is a separate document that supplies full details for the leaseholder on how to apply for permission to carry out these types of alterations. Available on application.

3. In all cases the porter or caretaker should be informed at least three days before the work is due to commence.

4. If the flat is to be unoccupied during the course of the work, a spare set of keys must be left with the porter or caretaker in case of emergencies.

5. The main door of the flat must be kept closed at all times while the work is in progress.

6. A clean adequate dust sheet must be provided to cover the area of the hall outside the flat and in some instances down the stairs. This can be agreed with the porter or caretaker subject to the nature of the work. The dust sheet should be laid out first thing in the morning before the work starts and removed in the evening and cleaned ready for the morning. Any residual dust or mess must be removed from the hallway, as soon as the dust sheet is taken up. Contractors are advised to have a vacuum cleaner on site.

7. The entrance doors to the building must NOT be left open and unattended under any circumstances.

8. Working hours for workers on site, unless otherwise specifically agreed with the managing agents, are 8.30 am to 5.30 pm Monday to Friday. Workmen on site outside these hours, at weekends, religious or bank holidays, will be told to leave immediately.

9. All contractors must have adequate insurance to cover loss or damage to other lessees' flats and common parts, as a result of their work.

Standard Conditions for Contractors

10 Noise, dirt and other nuisances must be kept to a minimum so as not to inconvenience other residents. Where the removal of plaster is involved all windows in the flat must be kept closed until the debris is removed.

11 Any work must not affect the common parts or their free use by other residents.

12 No transistor radios to be played on site.

13 All works must comply with statutory requirements.

14 Work must not affect or alter in any way the structure or layout of the adjacent common parts or any other flats in the block.

15 Water, electricity and gas. Works must not affect the supply of services to other flats except where mains supply is turned off to link up a secondary pipe or wiring. This must be arranged with the porter, caretaker or managing agents.

16 Waste disposal units. It is a statutory requirement that these must be plumbed into existing soil stacks. It is an offence to plumb them in to waste pipes or rainwater stacks.

17 New central heating flues, waste exits and ventilation grilles. Any proposed breaches in the external walls must be agreed with the freeholder before installation and MUST be cut with a core cutter and neatly repointed after the pipework or appliance has been fitted. New external pipework must be fitted in BLACK plastic (NOT grey, painted black).

18 Shower units must be tanked underneath with an external overflow pipe if practical; alternatively a shower tray with tiling upstands will be considered for approval. Tile bathroom floors should be laid with a waterproof membrane beneath the sand and cement screed with four-inch upstands under the wall tiles.

19 Disposal of builders' waste and old appliances:

   a Disposal of waste appliances is the responsibility of the leaseholder. Any costs involved in repairing damage, or carrying out extra cleaning in the common parts will be charged to the leaseholder. The builders should be warned by the leaseholder that any charges of this nature will be deducted from his invoice.

   b Light waste only can be removed in heavy duty plastic bags via the staircase and hallway.

c If a flat is on the ground floor, a window should be taken out to enable waste packed in heavy duty bags to be removed through the window and into the yard.

d The same technique can be used at first-floor level using a ladder, and at a second-, third- and fourth-floor levels using a scaffold and hoist. The use of scaffold requires permission of the managing agents.

e Where extensive areas of brickwork are involved, removal should be carried out with a skip in the yard. The siting of the skip must be specified and agreed with the managing agents.

f Redundant fittings and plastic bags of rubble can be stored for a maximum of seven days in the yard but only in a place to be agreed with and specified by the porter or caretaker and on prior specific removal arrangements being made and agreed with the caretaker.

g These arrangements apply unless an ad hoc arrangement is agreed with the managing agents because of specific problems.

Company name: *Date issued:*

APPENDIX 3

Welcome Pack and House Rules

The Welcome Pack should contain information which answers as many questions as a new leaseholder would be likely to ask. It should reflect the idiosyncracies of the building and contain those points of guidance and house rules that are currently in use. Rules governing the conduct of lessees already appear in the lease as the lessees' covenants. These may need improvement or interpretation either because they are in a form which is now partly outdated, or because the company has decided to exercise the landlord's rights under the lease to introduce additional rules. Certainly, most newly formed lessee-owned companies like to be seen to be making a fresh start, and a new, clear set of house rules issued under the terms of the lease helps.

Always imply that good practice is being encouraged and try to make the rule for positive reasons, that these rules are to protect rather than impel, for example:

> *'In order to maintain the smart appearance of the building, to prevent damage to its fabric and to discourage the lowering of the value of flats in the block, the display of agents' boards will not be permitted when a flat is being sold.'*

General information

- Caretaking/porter arrangements including relief duties
- Managing agent's details
- Insurance
- Telephone numbers:
    - caretaker
    - managing agents
    - entryphone
    - pest control
    - committee
    - board members

- Rubbish disposal
  - days
  - collection
- Parking
- Storage
- Keys
- Common parts use
- Common parts cleaning
- Balconies use
- Bicycles and other articles left on staircases and approaches
- Information on the disposal of heavy household rubbish
- Boiler houses, central heating and hot water
- Gardens
- Access to roof
- Method of payment for service charges and receipts
- TV aerials/cable TV/satellite dishes.

House Rules

- Noise and nuisance
- Subletting
- Structural alterations
- Bathroom and kitchen drainage
- Tidiness in the common parts
- Building works
- Cats, dogs, birds and other pets
- Overflows
- Floor covering
- Gardens, yards and enclosures
- Agents' boards.

Security and emergency

- Fire precautions
  - escape
  - alarms
  - equipment/extinguishers
  - drill
- Gas/water/electricity emergency
- Locksmith
- Lift failure
- Entryphone
- Flat security
  - doors
  - windows
  - balconies
- Address for legal notices.

It is a useful practice for one group to draft the information sheets and house rules and another to criticise the drafts until the wording is as clear and precise as possible. If the lease so permits, issue the house rules with the authority of the lease so that they carry that authority.

(Name of the company)   *(Date the rules were issued)*

APPENDIX 4

Formal notice requiring access

One of the most difficult aspects of a contract is coordinating access to individual flats in order to carry out essential repairs to windows and balcony doors. Some people will naturally be worried about strangers being in their flat in their absence and will require someone known to them, such as the caretaker, to be there if access is required. Other people remove their valuables for the duration of a contract and permit access.

Some leases state that the maintenance of the windows is the responsibility of the lessee; others say it is the landlord's. This will no doubt be taken into account when work is carried out to windows. For example, some companies bill lessees separately and therefore require frequent access to estimate and carry out the work. Others lump all the works together in the main contract. Whichever policy is adopted, the company must protect itself from complaints that works were not carried out when they should have been. The company, as landlord, will have rights of access under the lease and these it may decide to invoke. Others, understandably, put the responsibility for cooperation firmly on the shoulders of the lessees.

The following letter, which should be clearly dated, can be sent either by the company, by the contractor or by the supervising surveyor and can be amended appropriately.

(Name and address of supervising surveyor/contractor)

Dear........................

Re: External redecorations

This letter is to advise you that the company has appointed a contractor who will be carrying out works, in accordance with the terms of the lease, in the vicinity of your flat, that the work will begin in one month's time and will last about six weeks. During the period of the contract it will be necessary to obtain access to your flat in order to overhaul its windows. We would be grateful, therefore, if you could advise the site foreman as soon as works begin how access to your flat can best be arranged so that these remedial works may proceed with the minimum of inconvenience to you.

Formal notice requiring access

> If it is your wish that no works be carried out to your flat, please forward a copy of this letter to the supervising surveyor/contractor, whose name and address appear at the top of this letter, before the start of the contract.
>
> *Yours faithfully,*
>
> Please do not carry out any works to the windows of my flat for which I/we will remain responsible.
>
> *Name:* .... *Signature* ....
>
> *Flat:* ....

Index

A

Access
    formal notice requiring 201–202
Accountant
    fees 75
    services of 71–72
Accounts
    managing the 174–175
Advisory, Conciliation and Arbitration Service (ACAS)
    Employing People booklet
        information source 20, 29, 175, 187
    website 29, 175
Amenities
    managing 186
    objectives 116
    strategy 124–137
Annual General Meeting (AGM)
    agenda 188–189
    audited annual accounts 55
    checklist 189
    minutes of previous 55
    preparation 188
    proceedings 56
    report of directors 55
    resolutions for debate 55
    typical order of business 55
Anti-social behaviour
    difficult leaseholder 142–144
    subtenant 144–145
    unintentional offender 141–142
Appointing a Managing Agent
    free booklet 64, 76
Association of Residential Managing Agents (ARMA)
    Appointing a Managing Agent booklet 64, 76
    IRMA sponsor 64
    lists of members 65

website 64, 75
Attributes of block
generally 8

B

Block personalities
four 2–3
Building
checklist 103–104
contracts and specifications 162–171
description to be in lease 82
problems associated with 91–104
reading 104
works, conditions for leaseholders 190–194
Buy to let
problems with 145–146

C

Chairman
appointment of 41–42
importance of good 52
Committee of management
Industrial and Provident Society Act 1965, under 51
Committees
defining authority/activities 58–59
management
code of practice 60–61
generally 59
meetings 60–61
membership 59–60
purpose 59
meetings 58, 59–60
sub 58
terms of reference, defined by 58
working party 58
Commonhold
introduction of 1

Communality
    privacy, versus 149–150
Companies House
    annual return to 31, 189
    audited accounts to 189
    booklets 31, 50
    change of directors/secretary to 189
Company plan
    objectives
        amenities 116
        budgetary control 114
        checklist 123
        clearly stated, based on 105, 112–123
        consent for 118–122
        constraints on 122
        development of the property 114
        generally 113
        managerial performance 114
        planned maintenance 114–115
        services 116
        setting 116–118
        staff 115
    strategy 124–137
        amenities 131
        approaches to 125–126, 137
        checklist 137
        costs 131–132
        development of the property 128–129
        maintenance 130
        project based approach to 136
        purpose 124
        repairs 130
        reserve fund 134–136
        role in lessee-owned company 133
        rolling plan 126–133
        staff 131
Company secretary
    appointment of 42
    changes, effect of 189
Compliance
    problems 10

Consent
    obtaining
        generally 118
        LIP model 119–122
        transferable vote by 118
    problems 10

Contractors
    resource, as a 109–110
    Standard Conditions for 195–197

Contracts
    checklist 171
    defects liability period 169, 170
    employment of 177
    forms 165–166
    generally 164–165
    liquidated damages 170
    maintenance and service 182–184
    payment 169–170
    preambles 167
    preliminaries 166
    running 167–168
    scaffolding 163–164
    setting up 167–168
    specification 166
    stages in preparing/carrying out 166–169
    supervision 169
    surveyor, choosing 162–163
    works 167

Covenant
    enforcement 160
    landlord's
        lease, in 81
    lessee's
        breach, forfeiture for 16
        lease, in 81
    mutual enforceability 27, 78, 150, 160

D

Dampness
    action against 98–99

brickwork related problems 96
burst pipes, by 94–95
causes 92–93
condensation 97–98
consequences 99–100
creeping 93–94
generally 92
reading 104
rising damp 97
storms/damage by the elements 95–96
types 93–98

Decision-making
bodies
collective responsibility 51
generally 51
implementing 173–174
Location–Intensity–Priority (LIP)
device to assist 119–122

Dehumidifier
use of 99

Directors
appointment of 40–41
board of 51
full 39–40
changes, effect of 189
checklist 49–50
Companies House booklets 50
decision-making 57–58
duties
care, of 139
case law, founded on 44–46
statutory 56
duty of care
caring, distinguished 139
house code of conduct 46
individual, benefits of 42–44
meetings 56–58
committee procedure 56–57
typical agenda 57
powers 56
remuneration 56

Drainage
    problems with 149
Dry rot
    generally 99–100
    preventing 100

E

Employer
    duty of care 178
Expertise
    resource, as a 107–108

F

Federation of Private Residents' Associations (FPRA)
    address 14
    advice 65
        lease variation, on 78, 90
    membership 13
    website 13, 14
Fire precautions
    Fire Safety: An Employer's Guide 181
        availability 181
    generally 180–182
    notifying residents 181–182
    risk assessment inspection 180
Forfeiture
    breach of covenant, for 24–27, 143
    proceedings
        institution 16, 155–156
    Section 146 notice 24–27, 143, 151–152, 154, 155, 193–194

G

Ground rent
    collection of 16
    peppercorn, reduced to 79

H

Health and Safety
common law requirements 178
    non-compliance, effect of 178
Executive (HSE)
    website 180
    Writing Your Health and Safety Policy Statement 187
information on 180
inspection checklist 180
managing 178–180
risk assessment 179
statutory provisions 178–179
    non-compliance, effect of 179

I

Industrial and Provident Societies
members' checklist 50
statutory obligations 48–49

Information
landlord's requirement 17
RTM's entitlement 17–18

Institute of Residential Property Management (IRPM)
generally 64
lists of members 65

Insurance
broker
    commission 75
    services 73–74
lessee to pay excess 79

L

Landlord
access
    formal notice requiring 201–201
approvals 28–29
counter-notice by 17

covenant relating to insurance 79
existing contracts prior to acquisition 19–20
forfeiture by 16, 24–27
information requirements 17–18, 28–29
problems and solutions 138–161
    checklist 161
    reading 161
RTM, relationship with
    prior to acquisition 15–17
    rights of membership 16

Lease
abuse of
    leaseholders, by 141–144
    subtenants, by 144–145
approvals 28–29
appurtenant rights 82
building description 80
contents 21, 80–83
    introduction 80
    schedules 82–83
    sections 80–82
covenants 81
demised premises 82
determination 81–82
duration 79, 81
ground rent 81
initial purchase price 81
meaning 77
modern 79–80
    format 80–82
parties 80
problems 78
responsibilities, scope of 7, 20–21
service charges in 82
start of 77–78
structure 21, 80–83
traditional 79–80
    format 82–83
understanding 79–83
variation 78–79

LEASE
    See **Leasehold Advisory Service**

Leasehold Advisory Service (LEASE)
    information booklets 1
        Application to the Leasehold Valuation Tribunal – Service Charges, Insurance and Management 87, 90
        Appointing a Managing Agent 64, 76
        Appointment of a Surveyor/Management Audits 171
        The Leasehold Valuation Tribunal – a user's guide 87, 90, 161
        The Right to Manage 17, 29
        Service Charges, Ground Rent and Forfeiture 83, 90, 161
    website 29, 75

Leasehold enfranchisement
    introduction of 77

Leasehold Valuation Tribunal
    hearing 155, 156
    reference to 17, 18, 24, 25, 28, 87, 151–152, 154

Leaseholder
    abuse of lease by 141–144
    additional requirements
        bathroom appliances/WCs, installation of 192–193
        central heating installation, where new 192
        structural alterations 193
    application for building/alterations/improvements 190–194
        conditions for all categories 190–192
        permission requirements 190
    conflict between
        company involvement 159–160
        compromise versus collaboration 160–161
        constructive 160
        sources of 158–159
    difficult 142–144
    disputes between, responding to 150
        security of cost 150–151
    'post-buyout' 147
    unintentional offender 141–142

Lessee-owned companies
    And see **Right to Manage companies (RTMs)**
    appointment of directors 40–44
    assets 35–36
    planning strategy 124–137
    resources 105–110

types 2–3, 11–13, 30
> prestige block 2, 11
> substantial block/no managing agent 3, 12, 13

Local authority
> information, as a resource 112

Location–Intensity–Priority (LIP)
> device to assist decision-makers 119–122

M

Maintenance and service contracts
> boiler 183
> generally 182
> insurance 183
> lift 183–184
> pest control 182–183
> planning 184

Management
> assumptions 4–5
> background of 5–6, 7–104
> business of 6, 105–187
> companies 1
> experience
> > advantages/disadvantages 3–4
> routine 172–187

Management committee
> considerations 10–11
> experience
> > advantages/disadvantages 3–4
> generally 51
> objectives 9
> responsibilities 9–10

Managerial delegation
> principles 2, 67–70

Managing agent
> appointing a
> > free booklet 64, 76
> assessing work of 69
> choosing a 64–66

former
> information from, as a resource 111–112

managing 67–70
> delegating responsibility to 67–69
> generally 67

responsibilities 64

selection process 66

Meetings

advantages 52

Annual General (AGM) 54–56

chairmanship 52–53

checklist 62

committee
> meetings 58–61
> procedure 53–54

courteous behaviour paramount 62

decision-making 51

directors' 56–58

disadvantages 52

Extraordinary General (EGM) 56

generally 51

guidelines for running 54

problems encountered 54

shareholders'. *See also* **Annual General Meeting (AGM)**
> generally 54–56

types of 54–55

Memorandum and Articles of Association

contents 21

RTM
> amendments 33
> contents 21–22, 32–33
> obtaining a copy 21, 29
> purpose laid down in 112
> responsibilities, scope of 7, 14, 20–21

N

New resident

information to 147–149
> alterations, as to 147–149

drainage 149
generally 147

Nuisance
assistance in dealing with 161
difficult leaseholder 142–144
subtenant 144–145
unintentional offender 141–142

P

Planning strategy
amenities 131
approaches to 125–126
comparing 137
checklist 137
costs 131–132
development of the property 128–129
major projects 129
refurbishment 128–129
maintenance
contracts 130
planned 130
project based approach to 136
purpose 124
repairs 130
reserve fund 134–136
role in lessee-owned company 133
rolling plan 126–133
creating 126–128
model for three-year 127–128
staff 131

Professional advice
central to good management 63–64
checklist 75–76
choosing 74
code of conduct 63
fees 75
indemnity 63
meaning 63
need for, whether 70–71

resource, as a 110
types of 71–74
Protometer
use of 99

R

Reasons for buying/managing block
generally 8
order of priority 9, 14
Red Cross
First Aid course 180
Refurbishment of flats
conditions for leaseholders 190–194
Rent
profit, for
problems with 145–146
resource, as a 107
Reserve fund
application 134–136
model
external/internal refurbishment, for 135
purpose 134
resource, as a 106
Resident
amenities
managing 186
matters
managing 184–186
meaning 138
new. *See* **New resident**
occupancy irregularities 185
security 185–186
Resources
available 105–106
checklist 123
existing staff 108–109
expertise 107–108
former managing agent's information 111–112
local authority information 112

215

professionals 110
reliable contractors/tradesmen 109–110
rents 107
reserve fund 106
service charges 106
Right to Enfranchise (RTE)
introduction of 77
Right to Manage (RTM)
introduction of 77
Right to Manage companies (RTMs)
accountability structures 30, 37, 174–175
acquisition date 15
    checklists prior to 17, 18, 29
    duties on 22–23
    landlord's existing contracts 19–20
    problems/opportunities running up to 15–22
    relationship with landlord prior to 15–17
    responsibilities not transferred on 23–24
    service charges prior to 18–19
annual return to Companies House 31
approvals 28–29
assets 35–36
business plan 112–123
    aims 112
    objectives 113
Certificate of Incorporation 32
chairman, appointment of 41–42
Companies House
    booklets 31, 50
    information for small companies 31
company secretary, appointment of 42
constitution 15
costs 29
decisions, implementing 173–174
directors
    appointment of 39–44
    checklist 49–50
    code of conduct for 46
    duties 44–46
documents 32
duties
    generally 22–23

landlord informed, to keep 17
establishment
    Commonhold and Leasehold Reform Act 2002 (CLRA) 15
forfeiture process 16, 24–27
full board of directors, appointing 39–40
ground rent, collection of 16
incorporation 30, 32
landlord
    counter-notice 17
    forfeiture by 16
    membership of 16
    requirement to provide information 17–18
    rights 16
legal entity 32
limited
    guarantee, by 15, 34
    shares, by 34–35
management structure, deciding on 39
managerial components routine 172–187
meetings. *And see* **Meetings**
    first 38–44
    typical programme 173–174
Memorandum and Articles of Association 32–33
    amendments to 33
    contents 21–22
    obtaining a copy 21, 29
    responsibilities, scope of 7, 14, 20–21
notice of claim 15, 17
objectives 113–123
planning strategy 124–137
problems and solutions 138–161
reading 50
registered office 47
resources 105–112
responsibilities not transferred to 23–24
    forfeiture 24
    landlord-owned flats, for 24
    non-residential parts, of 23–24
rights
    information from landlord, to 17–18

        no-fault-based 15–16
        set up, to 15–16
  rules
        non-members and 34
  shareholders
        checklist 49–50
        leaseholders must be 78
  small companies
        Companies House information 31
  source of funds 36
  stationery 47
  structure 30, 36–38
        reality, in 36–37
        theory, in 36
  transfer of staff 20

Role of block management
  generally 7

Royal Institute of Chartered Surveyors (RICS)
  membership 73
  publications
        Service Charge Residential Management Code 83, 90

Royal Society for the Prevention of Accidents (RoSPA)
  website 180

S

Scope of block management
  generally 9–10

Security of cost
  rationale for 150–151

Service charges
  account, on 79
  acquisition, prior to 18–19
  allocation 85
  calculation 85
  checklist 90
  components 84
  consultation requirements 87–88
  disputes 87
  lease, in 82

    managing the 174–175
    non-payment, effect of 25, 151–157
        checklist 161
        financial leverage 156–157
        forfeiture for 155–156
        formal reminders 152–155
        hardship cases 157
    Notice of Demand 86
    policy 88–89
    reading on 90
    reasonable modern practice 79
    rent, treated as 79
    resource, as a 106
    RTM's main source of funds 36
    Statement of Account 86–87
    statutory provisions 83–84, 86
    trust status 88
    unpaid, interest on 79

Shareholder
    checklist 49–50
    meaning 35, 138
    service charges 85

Solicitor
    fees 75
    services 72

St John's Ambulance
    First Aid course 180

Staff
    communication with 177–178
    contracts of employment 177
    duties 177
    existing, as a resource 108–109
    managing 175–178
    materials/equipment 177
    objectives, setting 115
    pay 176
    performance 176–177
    planning strategy as to 131
    transfer to RTM 20

Structural problems
    generally 101–102

Subtenant
  abuse of lease by 144–145
  meaning 138
Surveyor
  appointment 171
  choosing 162–163
  fees 75
  services 73

T

Tenant
  meaning 138
  welcome pack 139–141
    advantage of 151
    checklist 161
    contents 198
    general information 198–199
    house rules 199
    security/emergency 200
Timber
  problems 102–103
Tradesmen
  resource, as a 109–110
Transfer of Undertakings (Protection of Employment) Regulations 1981
  existing staff, as to 20

W

Water damage
  flooding from adjacent flat, by 92